FINDING JOY IN THE JOURNEY

90 Day Journey to Healing

TABLE OF CONTENTS

From the Desk of the Grief Strategist

I love what I do, helping others share their stories and testimonies of healing from grief and loss. I have had many struggles with grief after losing both of my parents, all of my siblings to include 3 sisters and a brother, and the love of my life. The stories you will read on the pages inside of this book are individual testimonies of how they were able to find joy in the journey of grief. Grief is different for everyone. However, we are all connected by one word: loss. Each author shares their story of loss and God's redemptive power. Grief has a way of taking our joy away from us. This book was created to help you restore your joy, faith, and hope. My prayer is that as you read this, Joy finds you and overtakes you. "Finding Joy in the Journey" was inspired by my life and the journey to help others to heal from grief. Every word was fueled by the passion for healing and the will to persevere. My Mom was a visionary, so at a young age, I witnessed the ambition to go after more, to kick down doors, and to go above and beyond what was commonly expected. Faced with many obstacles and countless crossroads, I felt the necessity to share my experiences. In addition, there was a burning feeling inside of my heart to help others that may need that extra push or that nudge to become Authors. My pure intention is to inspire generations of visionaries to go after their dreams without wavering and understand the sacrifices they may endure. The 90 experiences you will read in *"Finding Joy in the Journey"* includes prayers, affirmations, and real-life lessons that will help you to rediscover joy after a life-changing loss. I give God all the honor and praise for this project. To the ladies and men of the collaboration, you all hold a special place in my heart. Thank you for being a part of my vision and helping others to *find joy in the journey.*

Vernessa Blackwell

DIEVAH ALLEN

Dievah Allen was born and raised in the nation's capital. As an Army Officer, she has served our country for the past 31 years. Although a military career as an officer was not her dream, it happened purely by accident and she just went with it!

Failure Builds Character

I am not saying this because I am in need, for I have learned to be content whatever the circumstances. I know what it is to be in need and know what it is to have plenty. I learned the secret of being in content in every situation, whether well fed or hungry, living in plenty or in want. I can do all this through him which gives me strength. Philippians 4: 11-13

While my military background serves me professionally, my true love is in the kitchen. I am passionate about the needs and satisfaction of my customers. I specialize in preparing mouth-watering culinary dishes with a southern flair. Throughout my military service, as well as cooking, I have learned that failure is necessary, but it does not mean its fatal nor final. Failure has allowed me to be successful in both of these areas of my life. Although I could not understand, I can honestly say that I am so much better for those failures. If anyone has ever tried to cook something for the first time, you know it can be an EPIC fail! Sometimes the ingredients are off and sometimes the chef is off, but either way, you learn and try again. Failure has allowed me to start over, many times. It allowed me to go back and see where I fell short. It has also provided me the opportunity to plan and organize so I can prevent the same mistakes from happening again Failure makes the victory of success even sweeter. I am the woman I am today because of my failures. Without it, I would never know what success feels like. Instead of fear of failure try faith! Acknowledge it. Embrace it. Try again! With myself, I can barely achieve anything, but with God ALL things are possible!

DIONNE ANDERSON

Dionne Anderson is a survivor. She is a Mother and a child of the Most High. She is a Personal Chef and Caterer specializing in healthy nourishment. Dionne is an 11-year breast cancer warrior.

Priceless Memories

He took bread, gave thanks and broke it, and gave it to them saying, "This is my body given for you. Do this in remembrance of me." Luke 22:19

I have been blessed to share time and space with special people whom I will always love and know they loved me. Gatherings for special occasions as well as no particular reason, have afforded me priceless memories of family members that I will cherish for life. Holidays, Sunday dinners, Friday fish fry, summertime cookouts, just to name a few. Every event and family get together commenced with food preparation and breaking bread together. In my own house, I attempted to bring that same vibe with every opportunity. I wanted my children to feel that love of family ties and enjoying simple things. Every meal I prepared had a story as to why I enjoyed it. My Mother was an amazing cook. I took issue with her adding meat to vegetables but otherwise always delicious and flavorful. Saturday nights prepping Sunday dinners are treasured memories. We had potato salad every Sunday regardless of what else was on the menu. Chop those onions and peppers "FINE". My sister Doris making club sandwiches cut in quarters. The bacon always perfect. My Aunt Cleo teaching me how to make pie crust. Uncle Jean ladling our bowls of bean soup with a wedge of day-old bread. Little Ryan making pasta with me. My Mother in Law, Celia, always had a pot of tender greens on the stove. Some kind of good eating. My sister Genevieve making peas and rice, rice always perfect. When I am feeling particularly melancholy and missing my loved ones, I prepare their specialties in their honor. When I bless my food, I thank God for them. I praise Him for sending a Comforter. Even through tears, I can smile because I know I will see them again.

RENEE ANDERSON

Renee Anderson is a native of Topeka, Kansas. Servant of God, Wife, Mother, Grandmother, and business owner of Health e' Hair & Skin Care Salon LLC.

Truth is the Struggle IS Real!

For no one is cast off by the Lord forever. Though he brings grief, he will show compassion, so great is his unfailing love for he does not willingly bring affliction or grief to anyone.
Lamentations 3:31-33

The Struggle IS real! This is not intended to glorify anyone's personal struggles, because we are all struggling with something. When we refuse to deal with the problems in our lives, we will face the consequences of having them surface in other areas of our lives. The Devil loves sinful secrets. How do you cope with the pressures of living a Holy Life during a crisis? One of the hardest lessons in life is letting go. Whether it is guilt, anger, love, loss, or betrayal, change is never easy. We fight to hold on and in the same struggle, we fight to let go. We want to heal, but never allow ourselves to heal. We continually hold onto it all in every conceivable way. Until we truly let the struggle become where we find our strength, it will remain a struggle. Only when we let go, will we find newfound respect, healing and, awakening for our souls again. Give your struggles over to God and receive your strength from Him. The struggle IS REAL, but God's strength to pull you out of your struggle is real too! Release your struggles to Him. In return, He will give you joy, love, strength, and peace everlasting.

A'LONDA "LONNIE B" BARBER

A'Londa L. Barber is a Mother of two, God's Servant and a published Author. She is the owner of Lonnie B Creative Designs where your vision is created and branded to become a reality.

Walking in Your Truth

For I know the plans I have for you, says the Lord. "They are plans for good and not for disaster, to give you a future and a hope."
Jeremiah 29:11

As individuals, we are so hard on ourselves. Striving to live up to expectations, prove ourselves and our worth can be exhausting. We have all have felt stressed, overwhelmed, and vulnerable at some point in our life. We are all striving to be better and doing the best we can. The question is, How often do we stop and ask ourselves, "Why do I do this?" After all, none of us are perfect. Since we recognize all these things, why is it so hard for us to be honest with ourselves, own who we are, where we are in life, and walk in our own truth? Jeremiah 29:11 reminds us that God loves us and He already knew the plans He had for us; they were of good and not for disaster. For us to embrace who we were created to be, we have to TRUST GOD, LOVE GOD, BE HONEST WITH GOD, AND ALLOW HIS WORD TO TAKE ROOT IN OUR HEART, so He can get us to the place where we love ourselves right where we are. Today, let us stand tall, never forget who we are, where we came from, and what we have gone through because those are the things that define who we are today. God is just waiting for us to surrender to His will and for us to walk on our truth.

GIL J. BEAVERS

Gil J Beavers is a lover of Christ, Husband, Father, Rich Relationships with Gil & Renée podcast host, and marriage mentor. Gil retired from the Air Force after serving 23 years and now holds a BA in Business IT Management from WGU and a premarital certificate with Prepare/Enrich.

Joy Got Me!

Consider it pure joy, my brothers and sisters, whenever you face trials of many kinds because you know that the testing of your faith produces perseverance. James 1:2

I was an 8-year-old boy when the news of my parent's divorce was delivered to my younger mind. "What did I do? Why can't he love me? Why am I not enough?" These three questions shaped how my heart saw itself and how I engaged with others. Until one day it did not. It was when I met her. In her eyes, I felt love. In her presence, I felt I was more than enough. With her what I do adds value. In her, my spark ignited a flame, together we put an end to our lifetime of shame. Together we committed to a lifetime of love and marriage, not rejection and pain. This new idea of life confronted my former experiences and caused my life to change. Today, this 52-year-old man is on a journey toward joy. I cannot erase my Father's choices. I can not undo my past. I am a man with purpose and that purpose will last. I live my life for Jesus. I love and serve Him in every way. Joy is my portion I am proud to say. Serving others is how I have learned to make the pain go away. Joy is my portion; it is the fruit in my life. Joy is my portion. It is the key to eternal life. I got Joy!

RENÉE M. BEAVERS

Renée M. Beavers is a Christ Lover, wife, mother, anthologist, podcast host of the Rich Relationships Podcast, and an App developer of Speak Freely with Gil&Renée. She is a five-time author and a passionate marriage coach & mentor.

The Pursuit of Joy

So with you: Now is your time of grief, but I will see you again and you will rejoice, and no one will take away your joy. John16:22

Finding joy is a life long pursuit for those of us who have been habitually disappointed as children. Joy is my greatest desire and my most passionate pursuit. Joy is the great neutralizer of disappointment. I have chosen to step over happiness and run into the arms of joy! Today I long to discover comfort in the power of joy. When things don't go as planned and when the people I love most do something I hate, joy infuses my heart and my life with peace. Happiness feels good, however, joy is choosing to trust our creator to find our identity and security in the evidence of His sacrificial love. Joy is not the absence of pain, disappointment, or broken-heartedness. In life, discovering and accepting joy is a journey. Hope is the vehicle that allows us to experience the benefits of living life in pursuit of joy. Joy is a journey, not a destination. Joy is a gift, not a possession. Joy is a choice, not an emotion. Amid my disappointment, joy clears the air. Stop and take it all in. Joy is a breath of fresh air. When joy comes on the scene, we are strengthened and renewed. We are transformed and changed. JOY will never leave you when happiness is nowhere to be found. JOY is our everything; in GOD's presence is where it can be experienced. Choose JOY!

DENISE BETHEA

Denise Bethea is a Mother, GlamMa, Sister, and Auntie. She is also a Preacher and Teacher of God's Holy Word and a lover of God's People. CEO of Women of Worth (WOW) EmPowerment and Worship EnCounter.

<u>The Gift of Joy</u>

But the fruit of the Spirit is love, joy, peace, forbearance, kindness, goodness, faithfulness, gentleness, and self-control. Against such things, there is no law. Galatians 5:22-23

Joy is the second listed fruit of the Spirit. How can we receive Joy? I am glad you asked. We just only need to receive it. Does this mean that we will not encounter any problems, sadness, issues, or concerns? Does this mean we will not encounter any challenges or hardships? It does not. Because we know that the Joy of the Lord is our strength; it does not matter what the situation may be; we can have this joy because the battle is not ours, it belongs to the Lord. God has the final say over any situation we may encounter. This gift of joy, which only the Lord gives, will keep us in peace (which is another fruit of the spirit) when things are good and when things are not. You see this kind of joy is not contingent upon our circumstances. If we let this joy sustain us daily, we will be able to deal with the vicissitudes of life. God is a keeper. If you keep your hearts and minds stayed on Him, we too can have this joy which is something the world cannot give us. We only need to decide to receive it, live in it, and it shall be ours.

TISNESHA BLACKWELL

Tisnesha Blackwell is a Mother of two lovely daughters and two amazing sons. She is an awesome daughter, sister, and supervisor.

Believe in God

Jesus said to her, "Did I not say to you that if you believe you would see the glory of God?" John 11:40

It is so simple to say, "I believe in God," than to actually believe in God. Do you believe in God, I mean do you believe in God to the extent that you would just trust that He wants the best for you no matter what or how you feel right now? Believing God means trusting God despite turbulent times. Believing God means trusting God despite the painful loss. If you believe God you will be ready to give your all, even what seems like your Isaac to show your love for God (Genesis 22). What does this imply? It means no matter who or what you have lost, it should not affect your love and affection for God. You will continue to believe God and to trust Him, even blindly that God knows best, and He desires only the best for you and your lost loved ones.

Prayer: I believe in you Lord Jesus, and I know that you will turn every sorrow and pain in my life to joy and rejoicing.

VERNESSA BLACKWELL

Vernessa Blackwell is a Mother and Grandmother. She is a 16-time author, book collaboration coach, Joy Restoration/ Grief Strategist, and motivational speaker.

<u>Joy, Unspeakable Joy</u>

Rejoice evermore. Pray without ceasing. In everything give thanks: for this is the will of God in Christ Jesus concerning you. 1 Thessalonians 5:16-18

Whether healing takes place or not depends a great deal on the choices we make along the way. The journey of grief is not a comfortable ride on an aircraft in which, once we are in transit, we have no responsibility until it is time to disembark. The journey of grief is more like a marathon over treacherous terrain. It requires personal commitment, great effort, and the willingness to experience pain. It requires strategy, pacing, endurance, and determination to reach the goal. Not everyone finishes the race.

It has been said that time heals all things. That just is not so. Many people never reach acceptance. For people of faith, a more accurate way to understand how healing comes about is – we will heal in God's time if we are willing to live in reality and to walk in faith. Our responsibility on the journey of grief is to find the will so that we may, with God's help, experience the grace to embrace the changed reality of our lives. The good news is *you can still find joy in the journey*, many have taken the journey of grief. Despite the risks and dangers, they have found healing. Much can be learned from their experiences. Following those proven steps that help you to rediscover joy after a life-changing loss.

ARTIANA BOLS

Artiana Bols is the Mother of two beautiful girls and a loving Wife. She is currently in college pursuing a degree in Dental Hygiene. She aspires to establish her own Dental Hygiene practice.

<u>When God Is Involved</u>

And we know that all things work together for good of them that love God, to them who are the called according to his purpose. Romans 8:28

When I first reflected on this scripture, the first message I got was that all "good" things work for the good of them that love God. I did not comprehend that it said "all things" both bad and good. It means some bad things can happen to me and God knows about it. Some pretty mean things can occur that will make me look like I do not have God by my side. However, those bad and mean things will turn out to be a blessing. How did I learn this? Simply from Jesus, our ultimate example. Jesus suffered death on the cross so He could win the glory He has right now. Jesus was humiliated and people even asked Him, "Where is your God?" Glory to God that our Lord Jesus knew despite the shame that followed would be the glory. Do you know this? Trust that God can turn that rotten situation of yours into a colorful cherry blossom.

Prayer: Father, give me uncommon faith to trust in your plan always.

CARMELA 'SISTAH' BOWENS

Carmela Bowens is a Mother, Grandmother, and SISTER! Most importantly, the daughter of The One True Living God. Carm is a LIFE PARTNER who loves helping others discover their FULL potential in their gifts, callings, and life.

Got Joy?

Delight thyself in HIM and your heart's desires are granted.
Psalm 37:4

Is **JOY** so lost that we have to find it? Where did it go? With the pandemic we face, so many people are down, discomforted, depressed, and socially distant. For liberty to be taken away and replaced by fear and torment their **JOY** is dim. **JOY** is pleasure and happiness. When trials and tribulations come to steal it, **JOY** can remain in the things you find pleasurable. David wrote: *Delight thyself in HIM and your heart's desires are granted. {Psalm 37:4}*

Losing my daughter, who I was still nursing, to a man (who didn't want to pay child support) and a pregnant lawyer who accepted filthy lucre over morality grieved me briefly, but my **JOY** was renewed when *counting it ALL JOY... {James 1:2}* finally resonated in my spirit. Belting daily, "I've got **JOY** like a river in my soul", (repeatedly) my **JOY** began to restore. Then I would proclaim: "This **JOY** that I have the world did not give it to me and the world cannot take it away," **JOY** began to fill my heart. *{John 5:11} says: That My JOY might remain in you and that your JOY may be full.* I have got **JOY** unspeakable, FULL of Hope, and FULL of GLORY! Gods' Great **JOY!**

BERNADETTE BUTLER

Bernadette Butler is a Wife, Mother, and Grandmother. She grew up in Chicago, Illinois. She is the author of, "Words of Praise, Joy, and Love", "Living with Autism - God, Me, and Melvin."

Walk with Me

"Come, follow me," Jesus said. Matthew: 4:19

I was quietly sitting in my garden when I felt the breeze of the wind brush against my face. I can hear the melody of music from the birds, I see flowers blooming in vibrant colors, bee's buzzing all around me and Hummingbirds humming. I saw footprints among the lilies. His voice whispered, choice. I rose and followed the sound. Where can I find you? Why can't I see you? "Walk with me", the words lingered in the air, "Walk with me." Can I find Him if I put my feet into the path that His feet will lead? Would I dare? "Come walk and follow me." How can I find you so I can be free? Look with the eyes of your heart, hear with your ears. Then your heart will open up and you will know, I am near. I opened His word and began to read. As His word began to flow in my heart I understood, He is near me and will never depart. I place my feet where He walked. The fragrance of His love filled the air. I closed my eyes and breathed Him in. I have given you all that you need. I have restored and unlocked your chains. I have set you free. Stay in the light and let the brightness of My love surround you. Each day I can find my Lord in His word. I placed my feet into His footprints and followed. I was quietly sitting in my garden. Feeling the breeze of the wind brush against my face. He said, "Walk with Me", I replied, "So let it be." My heart made a choice. I placed my feet into His footprints and my heart into His hands. I am resting in the rhythm of God's love.

CANDICE CAMILLE

Candice Camille is The Wellologist, Global Speaker, and Trainer. She helps women to become sexy fit & well through mindset, meals, and movement.

You Get to Decide

He gives power to the weak and faint, and to those who have no might he increases strength. Isaiah 40:29

Things may not have turned out quite the way you planned, but at any given moment you have the authority to say, "This is not how my story ends." You have the power to turn your pain into purpose. You must learn how to define your situation in a way that will empower you instead of it overwhelming you. Now is the time to "lean not" unto your own understanding. Let go and let God. We are responsible for our actions however, God chooses the outcome. Be careful of your choices especially in a time of anger and disappointment. Your consequences and rewards are a choice away. Choose wisely! No matter what happens, with God's help, you can always rediscover your joy. You have to decide to do better for yourself by taking care of your mind, body, and spirit. When life happens, you can depend on your faith and your body's equity to stand up for you in your moments of weakness. Remember that you are not being tested to show your weakness but to discover your power and strengths. Here is what I know for sure, better is always available if you want it. You get to decide.

RHONDA BERRYHILL-CASTANEDA

Rhonda Berryhill-Castaneda is an Early Childhood Educator, business owner, and children's book author. She is the Mother of two sons and one daughter and considers herself a Southern California native.

<u>Rediscovering Joy</u>

"Trust in the Lord with all your heart, lean not unto your own understanding. In all thy ways acknowledge Him and He shall guide your paths." Proverbs 3:5

Grief is the immense despair and excruciating pain we feel that is part of our journey of experiencing love. When we lose someone we love, it is gut-wrenching agony. We may believe the sorrow will never end. It feels as though we will never ever smile, laugh, or enjoy anything about life again. The days become sad, dark, and hopeless. The nights are unbearable. Grief is love. Experiencing grief is the other side of loving. Without deep love, we would never confront grief. When we suffer a loss, we are mourning the time cut short. We are never mourning the fact that we were able to show and share love with another. What has helped me tremendously is to practice being eternally grateful for the time we shared together. I use the word "practice" because it is not something that comes naturally as your heart is aching. Gratitude and scripture are what get me through. God has a plan for each of us and as painful as it may be, we must always be faithful and trust in the lord. Ecclesiastes 3:1-8 reminds us. *"For everything, there is a season, and a time for every purpose under heaven: a time to be born, and a time to die."*

MONIQUE CHANDLER

Consultant, Educator, and Author of "Reconnecting With Your Happy." Monique Chandler is a Distinguished International Toastmaster. She possesses a unique blend of contagious, high volume, motivational energy, and a sincere heart for helping others reach their pinnacle.

The Game Changer

Now may the Lord of peace Himself give you peace at all times and in every way. The Lord be with all of you. 2 Thess 3:16

For over three hours I was surrounded by a dozen bikers on Harley Davidson motorcycles. They surrounded my car as I drove back to Atlanta until I put my right turn signal on at Exit 115 off 85 North in Buford, GA. Once I exited, they did a U-turn and blew their horns at me. I drove into Preston Hills at Mill Creek Apartments at 7 a.m., Monday morning. I ran inside to quickly prepare for work. I had just sat on the side of my bed when the cell phone on my nightstand rang. My heartbeat accelerated because deep in my heart I already knew. "She just left us," Mom's voice quivered. My sister, Lisa, transitioned on April 8, 2002. We celebrated her home going service on April 13 with heavy hearts. Every year since then, I honor Lisa's love for college basketball by watching March Madness and attending the NCAA Women's Final Four. Our mutual love for college basketball bonded us and gave me a way to celebrate Lisa in a manner that I know is pleasing to her. Before her passing, I loved the moments we spent together. Her death became a game-changer for me. Now, March Madness is not just about basketball. It is a reminder of the special bond I shared with my brilliant, beautiful, and kind big sister, Lisa. And it is a reminder to always celebrate life today, for it is not promised to us tomorrow.

DIANNA KASPER-CRAWFORD

Apostle, D.D., of Cincinnati, OH, Pastor of Victory Deliverance Center is a Wife and Mother to seven children. She was born in Jamaica. She has been teaching and preaching God's word since 2001 and in full-time ministry since 2006.

God Is in The Midst of Our Grief

*Weeping may endure for a night, but joy comes in
the morning. Psalm 30:5*

Grief will find us at some point in our lives. It may come from losing a loved one to death, losing a job, depression, or rejection, to name a few. It comes suddenly without any warning, stealing our peace of mind and sending us in a fit of uncontrollable sobs. My marriage fell apart some years ago. We had some problems and I was praying and believing God to heal us and fix our marriage. It seemed we were moving in the right direction. Then one night I came home from work and he had moved out. I tried to hold it together for my daughter's sake. I did not want her to see me fall apart. The next day when she left for high school, my world came crashing down around me. I cried for days which turned into weeks. The grief I was so deep, I had a hard time shaking it. I knew Jesus wanted to set me free and I wanted His freedom. I needed to fix my eyes on Jesus. It is not easy to turn our sorrows over to God, even though He is there to console us. It takes time and patience. As believers, we are redeemed by the blood of the Lamb from this curse call grief. Each new day brings you closer to your healing. Hang in there, joy is on the way.

ERIKA BROWN-COLEMAN

Erika is the owner of ESL Enterprises. Erika is the proud Mother of three amazing young ladies. Erika is a co-author in 8 anthologies, a motivational speaker, and an ordained minister.

What Are You Collecting?

Your word I have hidden in my heart,
That I might not sin against You. Psalm 119:11

Do you collect things? There are things that I have purchased but have not activated them in my life. Why did you buy those books on the shelf that you never read and the tools and emails that are saved on your computer? For some reason, at some point, we felt like we needed them. We thought that they would be valuable to use, yet they are still being ignored. This is exactly what we do with the promises in the Word of God. We collect them. Psalm 119:11 states that we should hide the word of God in our hearts. But what is the purpose of hiding or collecting the promises of God if we are not going to apply them? The Word of God is a powerful, active tool that should be activated daily through prayer and worship. We are to take the Word off the shelf and apply it to our lives. Instead of worrying about the doctor's report or bills due, let us pull out our collections of the Word and activate them. Do you need healing? Activate Isaiah 53:5. Do you need finances? Activate Philippians 4:19. Are things uncertain in your business? Activate Deuteronomy 8:18. Some things were created for us to collect. The word of God is not one of them. It is active and was created to be hidden in our hearts so, in our time of need, we can activate it, apply it, and have faith that God will take care of us.

KHYEEMA FLEET

Khyeema Fleet is a recent graduate of Westlake Senior High School. She has been working at Food Lion. Her ultimate goal is to manage the Food Lion where she is employed.

Do Something Fun!

"So, I commended enjoyment, because a man has nothing better under the sun than to eat, drink and be merry; for this will remain with him in his labor all the days of his life which God gives him under the sun." Ecclesiastes 8:15

I have encountered lots of people who never overcome grief, people who never stand up after life has knocked them to the floor, people who want to stay down, stay sad, stay mourning, stay sorrowful, and stay gloomy. I have got good news for you, my friend. God says go out and have some fun. Go out and do something you love. Even if it is not for your own sake, but for the fact that God is telling you to do so. I want you to take note of the words, "under the sun". Do you know what this means? It means as long as you are in this world "under the sun", not under the ground, you have an opportunity to eat, drink and be happy! You are allowed to enjoy yourself by slipping out of that grief, out of that sorrowful outlook, cheering up, and enjoying all that God has given you in the way that pleases him.

Prayer: Dear God, I want to rise up from this position of grief and go out and have some fun just the way you want me to. Please LORD, give me the grace and wisdom I need to do this in Jesus' name.

DR. JUANITA FOSTER

Dr. Juanita Foster is an international speaker, consultant, and trainer in the area of leadership and team development.

Walk in Your Legacy Today

Beloved, I wish above all things that thou mayest prosper
and be in health, even as thy soul prospereth.
3 John 2:1

When a person hears the word legacy, they think about what they leave after their death or what is left to them. A legacy can be good or bad. When you look through the bible, you see who left a legacy; Abraham, King David, and most importantly Jesus himself. Think about it. Even Judas left a legacy.

As the new year rang into 2020, the thought of creating a lasting legacy is more at the forefront of my mind every day.

Whether you want to or not you will leave a legacy. It is up to you what kind of heritage.

Question: Can you walk in your legacy today? The answer is YES, you can! 3 John 2 confirms that we can.

What I love about this scripture is that it covers everything! God loves us so much that he wants us to not only create a legacy to leave but to walk in that legacy now. How do you walk in your legacy today?

We walk in our legacy by being clear and confident. Clear that God loves us and wants to be blessed, healed, and whole. Once we get clear about that, we become confident that our legacy will be one that leaves a lasting impression and honors God. Find scriptures that speak to the heritage you want to leave keep them before your eyes and in your mouth.

APOSTLE ANDREA M. FOSTER

Apostle Andrea M. Foster is a dynamic, sought after voice for the Kingdom serving numerous churches for the past 28 years. She is also a 26-year veteran and retired DC Army National Guard Deputy State Chaplain.

The Legacy Must Continue

Then Joshua built on Mount Ebal an altar to the LORD, the God of Israel, [31]as Moses the servant of the LORD had commanded the Israelites. He built it according to what is written in the Book of the Law of Moses-an altar of uncut stones, on which no iron tool had been used. On it, they offered to the LORD burnt offerings and sacrificed fellowship offerings. Joshua 3:30

The future of this country is secure only in the hands of those who hold regard for the historical past. It was George Washington that said, "We ought not to look back unless it is to derive useful lessons from past errors and to glean from those experiences." In the Bible, we find a dual attitude toward the past. Paul bids us to forget that which lies behind and press on to the future in Christ. We are challenged to consider God's dealings in the past to build towards the future. Insecure men and women try to destroy the work of those who went before them believing that their work is somehow new. People of more strength and confidence make every endeavor to weave what others have done into the texture of their own service and performance. Instead of following the crowd, Joshua knew the moral laws were key to the present and the future. For him what lied ahead was directly correlated to the legacy of Moses being grasped, applied, and written on tablets of enduring stone. He revived and reiterated Moses the lawgiver's words to the last syllable. This shows the character of greatness. Israel was always conscious of its history, built hope and courage, and endeavored to live upon the knowledge and understanding of it. Let us do likewise! Let us find hope in the sacrifices of our ancestors by remembering the past, take courage amid the present chaotic country, and endeavor to build upon this solid foundation in the future.

EVA FOUSHEE

Eva Foushee is a minister of the gospel, a Mother of four adult children, eight grandchildren, three great-granddaughters. She is an entrepreneur and a licensed insurance broker.

The Joy of the Lord Is Your Strength

Go and enjoy choice foods, sweet drinks, and send some to those who have nothing prepared. This day is holy to our Lord. Do not grieve, for the joy of the Lord is your strength.
Nehemiah 8:10

Although you have lost a loved one, it is not the end of the world. In Nehemiah, the eight chapter and verse 10 the Lord tells us to go and enjoy choice foods, sweet drink, and send some to those who have nothing prepared. He also goes on to say this day is holy to our Lord. Do not grieve for the joy of the Lord is your strength. God wants you to focus on helping others in your time of loss and always remember that this day right here, right now is holy to our Lord, and "The joy of the Lord is your strength." Now let us look at the 10th verse a little closer. "The joy of the Lord is your strength". Now if you take out of the verse (of the Lord) you will find (JOY IS STRENGTH).

DARKEMA FREEMAN

Darkema Freeman is a resident of MD, Mother of 4 and soon to be a Grandmother. She is a two- time best-selling Author.

What a Mighty God We Serve

*Come, let us sing for joy to the LORD; let us shout aloud
to the Rock of our salvation. Psalm 95*

The songwriter penned, "What a mighty God we serve, heaven and earth adore Him, Angels bow before Him, what a mighty God we serve." Do you believe you are serving a mighty God? Do you believe that God is the most powerful being? Do you believe that with God nothing shall be impossible? Do you know that God can change your destiny, He can reverse time, He can stop time, and He can do anything just to ensure you are happy and fulfilled in life? Do you realize that the Almighty God is not a liar and as old as He is, He has never failed? What would make you believe that this all-powerful and all-sufficient God would fail you, or has let you down?

Do not be offended in God because of three simple reasons;

1. He is so powerful, you cannot control Him.

2. He is so powerful, you cannot fight Him.

3. He is so powerful; He will do the unthinkable, just to make you smile.

Just continue to trust and depend on Him. Trust me, you will never be disappointed, I mean it never!

Prayer: God You are the Almighty God and I worship you. I trust and depend on you, please help me to always do so no matter what.

MATICE FREEMAN

Matice Freeman is a CSR in Washington DC. She is single, loving, and free-spirited.

Avoid Faith Killers

"Iron sharpens Iron, so one man sharpens another.
Proverbs 27:17

I remember in a sermon preached by Brother Kenneth Hagin he told the story of a woman who just lost someone close and was trying to stay positive and cheerful. But each time some new sympathizers came to see her, the sympathizers began to cry and wail and she herself will slip back into grief all over again. If you are struggling with grief or pain of any sort, you don't want to be surrounded by people who will not help your faith, but by people who will build on whatever strength you have, by people who will speak God's truth into your life. The more words of faith you hear, the more encouraged you will become, the more you see strength in others, the more strengthened you will become. Try limiting your exposure to whatever kills your faith and surround yourself with faith tools.

Prayer: LORD, send people and resources to me that will help build my faith and strength to go through each day in Jesus' name.

APRIL GREEN

April Green is a Wife and Mother of three children living with Autism Spectrum Disorder. A licensed minister, special educator, and two-time international best-selling author.

In Your Grief Cry Out to God

I call out to the LORD, and He answers me from his holy mountain.
Psalm 3:4

When faced with the different emotions of grief that keep us down in a dark place, we need to remember to cry out to the Lord and call on Him. The God we serve is bigger than any grief or sadness that we are grappling with. Grief can cause us to lose faith, lose hope, and harden our hearts. During your time of sadness and grief, harden not your heart. Cry out to the Lord, He will comfort you. He will deliver you from your anguish and fill you with joy. He will guide you. He will give you peace to continue your faith walk in Him. When you cry out to God, He can hear you. Even if you cannot get the words out of your mouth, God can search your heart. Through the power of the Holy Spirit, He understands your moans and groans that are crying out to Him. God hears the cries of one tormented on the inside with grief. He hears the cry from within of pain and helplessness. From our cry, the chains of grief and sadness are broken and we are made free. Free to heal, love, and be free to live our lives knowing that God does not give us pain without relief or sadness without joy. As you navigate from grief to peace in your journey to find joy remember God is always with you.

LAKEISHA TRIMM-GREEN

LaKeisha Trimm-Green is a Veteran, Mother of 4, and Grandmother of 3. She graduated from Houston Community College with degrees in Health, Business Administration, and Medical Front Office.

Today Is My Day

With men, it is impossible, but not with God; For with
God, all things are possible. Mark 10:27

Today begins the last day of my life. I am giving myself to God to continue my journey with Him. Today will be the day to lay it all on the table and let go of all negative things. Knowing that I have a lot of baggage I carry and seem to always add more, today I am vowing to not add more. I will allow the spirit to guide me every step because I know it will lead me on the path God wants me to go. My family and I will be better mentally, spiritually, and emotionally when we give it all to Him and follow his purpose for our lives.

I have forgiven those who harmed me in my past and I have detached myself from them. I relinquish all the anger that I may have and pray for inner peace in order to be there for my loved ones that need me most. I will continuously pray for creative energy so that it will guide me to more brilliant ideas for the goals that I have set.

Today, I abandon my old habits and change to more positive and productive ones. I am blessed with incredible children and grandchildren. I will acknowledge my own self-worth daily; my confidence is improving. God sends us through these challenges to keep us on the path He wants us to go.

The obstacles that were placed to make me fail are moving out of the way and allowing God to fulfill His purpose in my life and push me towards greatness.

GLORIA GARCIA-HARRIS

Gloria Garcia-Harris is a Teacher. Gloria has a Bachelor's in Arts and a Master's in Educational Psychology with Emphasis in Bilingual Education.

<u>Grieving from Within</u>

He is the Healer of the brokenhearted, and the One Who
binds up their sorrows. Psalms 147:3

And there you lay, grieving a loss so personal… so painful, grieving yourself. The man, woman, person you were before. Before the diagnosis, before the accident, before the injury, before the moment everything changed. That person could stand, walk, run, write, laugh, feel, learn, hope. You miss that person. With the scars, the illness, the disability, the pain, and the emptiness. Many are grieving the loss of a loved one, grieving after a divorce, grieving the loss of a job, grieving after we lose a family pet. But there are those of us who grieve ourselves. We are unable to explain our grief, worried that we might sound selfish or ungrateful. At least we are still alive. You and I are somewhere in here my friend, your pain, the emptiness that rocks you to your core is real. You are not alone. Behind you are many more people who have lost themselves in a matter of moments. I am writing as one of these people. I understand. I do not know your story and you do not know mine, but what I do know is that beauty can grow from this dark place. Every stage of grief applies to this loss. Remember, life is a journey and it matters what we make of it. The questions that will help determine growth are; Did we learn from it or not? Are we wiser or not? Are we stronger or not? Do we love ourselves more or not? Love in our hearts for ourselves and others can change the world!

EVANGELIST LAWANNA HARROD

LaWanna Harrod resides in Maryland with her beloved husband. They have two sons and three grandchildren. Harrod is also a psalmist, CEO of Harrod Publishing, Harrod Photography, and Christian Sistahs.

My PerSistance Story

In times of trouble, He will shelter me; He will keep me safe in His temple and make me secure on a high rock. Psalm 27:5

How is a person supposed to release themselves from the emotional capture of years of molestation, abuse, feelings of worthlessness, confusion, and low self-esteem? This will require time to process the truths that are revealed. We are all on an intense journey to take action for what we have shelved in our hearts and minds. It will require us to confront the past and encourage transformation, healing, and wholeness without a lot of psychobabble and technical terms or theories. We must get to the healing spot! The signs and symptoms we have accumulated must be handled with a step-by-step approach for those who want to remove the junk and journey on in life with a lighter load, free from the pain and clutter of yesterday's history. I have written several books that cover a range of topics, all designed with the use of self-realization to release you from your self-imposed bondage. As we journey to seek out the root cause of our hindrance by faith, we must firmly believe in a favorable outcome. We all must go through spiritual healing and foster growth within oneself while helping recognize hurts and pains. We do all of this with the intent to cultivate your pain and transform your perspectives into the building blocks for your life. When I first started writing, I did not anticipate the depth of my well-hidden memories to surface so hard and so fast. The personal adept exploration and sharing of my experiences have led many to find the courage to confront their inner emotions and effectively lead others toward resolving those barriers. All I knew was I had to get there, and you can too. There where? The healing spot.

AFRIKUS HART

Afrikus Hart, LPN, a certified substance abuse nurse who assists those who struggle with addiction using a holistic approach.

I Forgot My Why!

But He said to me, "My grace is sufficient for you, for My power is made perfect in weakness." 2 Cor 12:9

I have been working in substance abuse for over a little over 13 years now and along the way, my heart was hardened towards the people I serviced. Along the way, I had become discouraged and desensitized to the struggle of those who have difficulty in maintaining sobriety. In my daily interactions, I found that (plus it was pointed out to me) I was being mean and very judgmental towards my clients. I prayed & had to take a step back to look at my actions and see that my purpose is to help, and I was doing more harm. I work in recovery and addiction to honor my dad who struggled with addiction, I couldn't help him because he wasn't ready and he needed more than just medication to succeed and now I have the tools to assist those in need. I feel proud today because I am not doing something just because I can, I am doing something to help someone and make a difference in their life. Sometimes in life, we can become hardened in our environment, but you cannot allow that to let you lose focus of your purpose or your goal and never forget your why. As long as you remember your why you cannot go wrong. My why is my motivation to do better. What is your why? Appreciate where you are in your journey, even if it is not where you want to be. Every season serves a purpose.

APOSTLE RENATA HENDERSON

Apostle Renata Henderson is the founder of Plan A Global Ministries, REACH U, Inc., & Life with Nata.

Shell Shock

Yea though I walk through the valley of the shadow of death,
I will fear no evil: for Thou art with me; Thy rod and staff
they comfort me. Psalm 23:4

Shell shock is defined as a psychological disturbance caused by prolonged exposure to active warfare, especially being under bombardment. It is a feeling of severe shock or surprise. Often used to describe those who have gone through war and fought in the military. While I would never diminish the sacrifice of those who experienced this physically, it was the only term that could truly explain what I was going through in mid-2016. I was in a war for my soul. The enemy of my soul was pulling all stops. I experienced so much loss that year. I lost the man I loved in January. I lost my *"still young enough to live"* sister, who died at the age of 46, in April. I lost a woman who was like a Mother and mentor for me in June. I lost my house after being laid off and fighting as hard as I could to keep it. I even lost my gallbladder! I thought I was going to lose my mind. All the while, the Lord was whispering to me glimpses of my destiny. I was so low. I begged God to take my life. I hoped He would answer my cries to let me die, without committing suicide. I was beyond a state of grieving. I was officially in "shell shock". There was only one answer to these questions that seem to have no answer-Love. Amid some of the most terrible situations of my life, the Lord showered me with so much love, that it melted my numbness and began to will me back to life. All that mattered was God was with me every step. As long as He was with me, life's trials seemed bearable. I let the impact of the lives who were no longer with me in the physical, impact how I make decisions for those I would still be able to impact. God gave me the will to live again, but their deaths impacted how I chose to live: dangerously free.

LASHAUNDA C. HOFFMAN

LaShaunda Hoffman is the author of Building Online Relationships; One Reader at A Time. She also created Shades of Romance Magazine; a digital magazine for readers and writers of multicultural literature that celebrated 20 years online.

Find Joy in Writing

Gracious words are a honeycomb,
sweet to the soul and healing to the bones.
Proverbs 16:24

Can you find your writing joy in grief? While you are going through grief you do not feel like you will ever find joy in writing again, but it sneaks up on you and wraps you tightly. After my Mother died, I was on a hard path to finding my writing joy. My characters were not talking to me. My muse was stuck. As a writer, I am also a researcher, so I started researching grief and how it affects you. I learned many writers going through grief had a hard time writing again. I decided to share my experiences with grief through a blog series about how I dealt with the grief of losing my Mother. It gave me the joy I needed to be able to put all those feelings down so I could release them from my spirit. I hoped it would help someone on their grief journey. To my delight, one of my good friends said my words helped her understand her husband's grief. The joy of helping someone melted my heart. As I worked through my grief my characters began to talk to me again. It is such a joy to create characters and stories. I am thankful I was able to find my writing joy again I just had to give it time. Just keep on living are words my Mother used to say to me. Just keep on living and you will find new joy every day.

BRANDY HUNT

Brandy is a native of Greenville SC and the Mother of 1 daughter. She is a 6-time Author, Publisher, Corporate Trainer, Life Coach, and Motivational Speaker.

Lay Aside Every Weight

Trust in the Lord with all your heart and lean not on your own understanding; in all your ways submit to Him, and He will make your paths straight. Prov 3:5

Disappointment can weigh us down. Before we know it, we are complaining more and moving by faith, less. Where does this disappointment come from? It could be past trauma, abandonment, rejection, or just one of life's unfortunate circumstances. When life has dealt you a bad hand, the last thing you want to do is hand your life over and trust God. Life happens with or without our permission. That means both good and bad. Events like losing a home, a job, or even the death of a loved one can leave a feeling of disappointment that tries to linger long after it should have already passed. Grief. It's a natural response when an expectation has not been met, however, if you find yourself unable to move past a certain event or experience, you may need to lay aside the weight of disappointment and trust in the Lord again. God knows more than we do. We must trust, even when the answer is no. We cannot trust God and question his leading at the same time. We must fully lay aside our own will and continually allow Him to show us His will. Disappointment may come, but you can quickly dismiss it by reminding yourself, "I trust in the Lord and He will direct my path!" If the Lord is directing your path, what reason do you have to be disappointed forever? None. It is natural to be disappointed if something does not go quite the way we plan it, but we do not have to stay that way. We can choose to move past our pain, hurt, disappointment, and insecurities. There is a brighter day beyond all the dark clouds. There is promise and hope past our pain. There is joy for the journey ahead regardless of the circumstances that we may find ourselves in.

DEBORAH IVEY

Deborah Ivey is a Mother of two adult daughters, Wife, Grandmother of two granddaughters, Author, and a US Army retiree. Deborah co-authored 4 books.

<u>Coping and Healing</u>

***With man this is impossible but with GOD all things
are possible. Matthew 19:26***

There is a light at the end of the tunnel. I lost my brother in 2000, my Father in 2005, my Mother in 2014, and my Mother's boyfriend in 2015. Those were some trying times. I had to stay busy and keep my mind occupied otherwise I would have been a nervous wreck. I like to read romance books, travel to different places, and write so those things helped me with my grief. You have to tell yourself that this too shall pass and that you can get through this by taking one day at a time. It will not always be easy, but you can do it. You have to jump out there and enjoy life because you are still amongst the living. Your family would not want to put your life on hold for them. Father, I come to you on bended knees asking you to help me when my grief gets the best of me. Father, I need you right now so I can see my way clear.

Father, you said you would never leave me nor forsake me. I thank you for all the things you are doing any my life. Sometimes I do not understand but I know you had a reason why you called them home. Quiet my mind when I get weary. I am asking all these things in your name, Amen.

CHRISTINE JACKSON

Christine is a Wife, Mother, and Minister of the Gospel. She is the founder of Torch of Hope, Inc; a 501c (3) non-profit organization whose mission is serving survivors of crime victims and those who have lost loved ones.

Generations Are Waiting on You

You will be secure because there is HOPE;
You will look about you and take your rest in safety.
Job 11:18

As we take the rigorous, painful, and uncertain Journey of Grief, we can take comfort and be rest assured that our loved one(s) are at peace. We all must go through the cycles and emotions of the Grief process for a healthy exit from the Valley of the Shadow of Death. It is not uncommon to repeat the cycles of grief. As we pass through this valley of pain, hurt, sorrow, and loneliness, remember that we are not alone. God is with us. We may ask ourselves. "Will I ever smile and enjoy life again?" Yes, we will. We will meet and talk with others along the journey who either are walking through the grief process, were transformed through it, or are currently facing it. It is through our loss, that sharing our story with others who are struggling and without hope that God will continue to provide us the strength to continue living our lives to the fullest. God will take our gifts, talents, and abilities and use them in ways we have never imagined, to encourage His children who have been overtaken with losing their loved one(s). Let us be encouraged and surrender our broken pieces unto the Gracious Lord and Savior Jesus Christ and He will surely turn our mourning to joy. Currently, our nation faces the most critical times and people are dying everyday. Allow the Peace of God to provide joy so that He may equip us to evangelize hope in Jesus Christ to those hurting and suffering loss and grief in silence.

MARITZA JACKSON

Maritza Jackson is an Independent Consultant and Mom to 3 beautiful children. She has a passion for health, wellness, and expressions through the written word.

Thankful Appreciative Gratefulness

Love is kind; love does not envy; love does not parade itself, is not puffed up; does not behave rudely...; bears all things, believes all things, hopes all things, endures all things. Love has no fear; love...never fails. 1 Cor. 13:4-8

I'm wishing you were here to hug, my dear. I'm feeling you here in treasured moments and near in my precious memories. I feel you keeping your presence alive, not only in my heart but also in my mind.

Thank you for leaving so many reminders to hold my soul together. I'm so appreciative of this love and how it is helping me pick up the pieces of my heart.

On my hands and knees, this feeling of incredible love and gratefulness caresses my soul; it stabilizes my mind so that I can pray.

Thankfully, Appreciatively, Gratefully, I pray from my heart, with my whole-mind and spirit-filled-soul: Dear God help me, please!

Thank you so much for your love. Your faithful words comfort and hold me. I know that you will not leave me. Dear God help my aching heart. Thank you for reminding me of love! It holds the key to my healing.

I know that you love me. Dear God, help my anxious soul. Thank you for your grace, mercy, and undeserved loving-kindness. How wondrous, to have so many powerful memories, tucked away inside for such a time as this.

Heavenly Father, I am truly Thankful, Appreciative, and Grateful, for you allowing me a place to focus and a space to pour all that I feel for my loved ones.

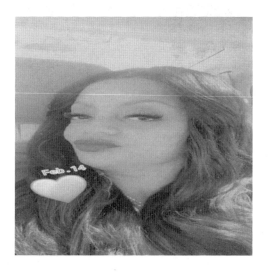

LAKEISHA JENNINGS

Lakeisha Jennings, a native of North Carolina, studied at UNC and graduated from Orange High.

Cultivate a Habit of Praise

"I will bless the LORD at all times, His praise shall continually be in my mouth." Psalm 34:1

Praise is always a powerful tool in chasing away despair, grief, sorrow, pain, or bondage. That notwithstanding, it is not easy to praise. You might say, "But how? I mean praising God is easy and I do it always." Well, if you take a good look at our scripture for today, it says "bless the LORD at all times", whether things are good or bad, whether it is convenient or not convenient. It says all times we should always be praising God. Dear brother, dear sister, we have a responsibility to praise and worship God all the time until it becomes an addiction. That is when it gets to a point whereby if you do not praise God, you feel uneasy. When we learn to do this, our cup of joy will never run dry.

Prayer: Jesus I praise you today for my life, for my family, for my nation, for all you have done, all you are doing, and all you are yet to do. Continually Lord, please give me the grace to always praise you and be grateful.

TASHA JENNINGS

Tasha Jennings is a loving Mother and Grandmother. She is an addiction survivor; 15 years and counting. She holds an occupation in Behavioral Health.

I Trust God Until the End

Shadrach, Meshach, and Abednego answered and said to the king, O Nebuchadnezzar, we are not careful to answer thee in this matter. If it be so, our God whom we serve can deliver us from the burning fiery furnace, and he will deliver us out of thine hand, O king. But if not, be it known unto thee, O king, that we will not serve thy gods, nor worship the golden image which thou hast set up. Daniel 3:16-18

Wow! I really love these guys from our scripture reading. We need people like this in our military. Two things determine loyalty. Trust in whom you are loyal to and the willingness to die for their cause. That was exactly what Shadrach, Meshach, and Abednego expressed, they trusted that God would deliver them, and then they prepared their minds that even if He does not, they were willing to die for their beliefs. We must all learn to trust God till the end, to trust Him no matter how dark it might seem right now. By trusting God, you save yourself a lot of stress and burden, which helps ensure your days are filled with joy and without continuous sorrow which leads to depression.

Prayer: I will trust you to the end O LORD, the grace to stay faithful in this please grant unto me in Jesus's name.

CHRISTINA JOHNSON

Christina Johnson, also known as Crissy the Momcologist, is a Certified Life Coach, Motivational Speaker, Author, and childhood cancer advocate.

Healthy Ways to Navigate Grief

He refreshes my soul. He guides me along the right paths
for His name's sake. Psalm 23:3

Grief at times is overlooked and the people experiencing it tend to ignore the feeling or simply ignore the fact that they are grieving. When my one-year-old son was diagnosed with cancer I went through several stages of grief. I found myself in a dark hold. I often isolated myself which made it harder to overcome the grief that I was experiencing. There is no natural remedy to the feelings or a process to learn and employ when one suffers from grief hence the need to not overlook the grief process but to actually learn how to overcome the situation. For me, I had to first accept the fact that I was grieving. Self-acceptance is a part of the self-healing process. Once this occurred, I was able to pull myself slowly and gently out of the isolation mode I was in. I located a local support group that I attended. This brought comfort for me as well as others as they were able to relate to me. We were able to form a healing process that is so strong due to the togetherness in times of need. I also engage in healthy activities such as crying are a sure way to ease the situation from the bondage of the grief. I also found help from reading the bible and praying. This helped me develop a strange level of faith which help me process the grief.

REV. DR. PATRICIA A. JOHNSON DOWTIN

Rev. Dr. Patricia A. Johnson Dowtin was born in Washington DC. She achieved a Bachelor of Business Administration from National-Louis University and a Master of Divinity Degree and a Doctor of Ministry Degree at Wesley Theological Seminary in Washington, DC.

Fear or Faith

For God has not given us a spirit of fear but of power,
and love, and a sound mind. Timothy 1:7

Do you know what issues in your life caused a spirit of fear to attempt to overtake you? Issues of life, such as a lack of financial resources? The death of a loved one? A serious illness? A pending divorce? The loss of your job? Aging and alone? Enduring domestic violence from the hands of the one who is supposed to love and protect you? Is someone you love incarcerated? There are many more issues I could add to the list. None of those situations were invited into our lives, yet we have all experienced one or more of them. Unfortunately for me, I have experienced each one of them at one time or another. For those who are still young and have not yet experienced any of the above issues, get ready because life happens to all of us, and as sure, as our hearts beat, you shall encounter one or more of them. For me, *Finding Joy in the Journey* was the opportunity for an understanding and a revelation that God is who He said He is. When Moses asked God, who should I say has sent me? God's answer was, and still is, "*I AM, THAT I AM!*" The great "*I AM, THAT I AM*", is our Father, God. He who shall never leave us, nor forsake us. He loves us more than we love ourselves. That true/deep love from a Mother or a Father for their child is the closest example I can use for how God loves us. As His children, it does not matter what issues we encounter or what we must go through, we are not alone because our Father, God, is in the situation with us! When that spirit of fear attempts to destroy you, rise in faith and say: "*God has not given [me]a spirit of fear, but [He has given me the spirit] of power, and love, and a sound mind.*" Amen.

LANEIKA R. JOHNSON

LaNeika R. Johnson is a devoted Mother of twin girls, Army Veteran, Travel Agent, Entrepreneur, and most, importantly, a Woman of God.

<u>Finding Joy in Shame</u>

Consider it pure joy, my brothers and sisters, whenever you face trials of many kinds because you know that the testing of your faith produces perseverance. James 1:2-3

As one year ends and another begins, we often find ourselves ready to embark on new journeys and resolutions by developing plans to accomplish our goals. As Christians, we know that we are new creations in God (2 Cor. 5:17, NKJV). Finding Joy amid a life-changing experience, here is my journey to Texas! I moved to Texas hundreds of miles from my church and biological family. I knew it would be an adventure, but not like this. Shortly after arriving, I found myself, pregnant-with twins! Single, saved, pregnant, and ashamed I had gotten myself "here," I worried about what others thought and how I would get through it. Feeling I let God down and ultimately defeated, I lost all Joy. Fortunately, God sent women of God to speak into me, reminding me of His Word deep inside me. I knew then even in "this," God yet chose and loved me. Remembering His willingness to forgive my sins, I repented, asked God for forgiveness, knowing my sins were washed away. Finally, I found Joy in my pregnancy. Learning the importance of finding joy in motherhood, my faith in the Lord was vital. Daily I chose to consider it pure Joy that whatever trials came my way was merely a test of my faith, which ignited my perseverance. When making God our hearts' Joy, adding faith, and growing our relationship with Christ, then we can genuinely have Joy. Choose God to have the Joy that only He can give!

MARQUITA KENNEDY

Marquita Kennedy is a prayer warrior, Mommy, strong, tithing, Woman of God. She is an educator, friend, mentor, roller-skater, poet, chef, and a financial analyst.

Judge Not

Judge not according to the appearance but judge righteous judgment. John 7:24

For many have fallen short of the promises of our Lord,

What shall one believe when the reality pierces through like a sword?

You try so hard to live right and do what is best,

But the sheep in wolves' clothing always seem to know no rest.

It is ok to make mistakes and it is ok to lose no hope,

The fight that is within you shall not be the end of your rope.

Why do so many fret over what other people may say,

This is your life to live and we are granted the same 24 each day.

Keep your head held high because this too shall pass,

How does one look down upon another, such a low class?

In these days and times ahead, you have the ability to re-write this phase,

Overcoming each obstacle that has you barricaded as you are in a maze.

Roll up those sleeves and get your feet steadfast in the boldest spot,

God is your Vindicator and onlookers will honor your strength & JUDGE NOT…

BRITTANY KING

Brittany King is a Mother of four young kings and a woman of God. She is an aspiring memoirist and author. She is also a mentor and role model to all you g women. Her journey to motivate young ladies has just begun to flourish.

I Know Who I Am

A wife of noble character who can find? She is worth far more than rubies. Proverbs 31:10

I used to be weak and insecure! I used to be scared to dare to be bold! I had an attitude out of this world, but no real voice outside of anger! I constantly watched others do all that I wanted to do. Yet, too fearful of being viewed as trying to be like the rest! I always dimmed my light to let others shine brighter, even though my bulb was just as bright! But baby, it is something about the number 30! Sprouting and rising to who God has called me to be, happened for me at 30! A sense of peace, a sense of security, a sense of self-love, a sense of KNOWING WHO I AM! Today I walk in purpose! All that I do is intentional. I will continue to allow my light to shine! When I walk, in my mind the ground shakes! This walk is packed with power! When I say move to whatever mountain is before me, it moves because God gave me the AUTHORITY to make it happen by Faith! When I look at myself in the mirror, I remind myself that I am created in the Lord's image! Daily I wink at myself in the mirror, blow myself a kiss, speak over my life and say "Hey girl hey, you got this! Royalty she is! Phenomenal I am and so are you!

ELECIA BROWN-LEWIS

Elecia Lewis is a Wife of 20 years, a Mother of 2 angels on earth, 2 angels in heaven, 2 bonus children, and a daughter. She has been an entrepreneur, a stay at home wife, and a caretaker of families during their end of life's journey.

Victorious Not a Victim

The LORD is close to the brokenhearted and saves those who are crushed in spirit. Psalm 34:18

A Mother's worst fear is losing a child; having lost two began to put my life in a different bracket. I love different, I care differently, I hurt different and I mourn differently. There is no right or wrong, you cannot put a timeframe on feelings or grief or even know if you will ever smile again. Losing someone close to you gives a bigger meaning to the word Faith, as you keep the memories and cherish the moments while trying to stay in peace; You should stay focused on the only unchanging factor in your life that keeps you purposeful. The whispers of God. When God is speaking, he is speaking new life into you as you mourn, and that new life is oftentimes a fragment of the lost loved one's life that was designed to move through you on your path of being *victorious and not a victim*. Stay in peace and listen.

PASTOR TAMELA LUCUS, EDS

Tamela Lucus is Author of "Pompi-You Are Love" and "How I Feel on Any Given Day." She is a Mother of nine, Grandmother of six, Preacher, Teacher, Singer, and Songwriter.

When I Was Nothing, God Loved Me

Even though I walk through the darkest valley I will fear no evil, for you are with me; your rod and your staff, they comfort me. Psalm 23:4

When I was lost, He cared. Sometimes it seems like we are walking through the valley of death, full of decisions and misunderstandings. But God knows and sees everything. He cares for us even when we want to give up and say, "I cannot take it anymore." God has made us strong and wise as eagles. Regardless of our position in wealth and fame we still need you, Lord. To guide us and help us all the way. Lord, when I am in doubt, send someone my way to love me. If no one comes let me be like Paul. He said I have to encourage myself sometimes. Lord let me never get to the point in which I cannot lean on you. When I really need help, give me a mind to seek help and not care what others think of me. For my mind and body belong to you, Lord. I am here to give you praise and worship with my whole heart. Cover me, cover my children, cover my grandchildren, and the children to come. Bless us with a long life. Allow us to have favor with you and man.

BEATRICE MOORE LUCHIN

Beatrice Moore Luchin is an ordained Minister, dedicated Wife, Mother, and Grandmother who uses her experience as a lifelong educator, Author, and business owner to share the Gospel of the Lord beyond the church walls.

Wake-Up Worry Free

When anxiety was great within me, your consolation
brought joy to my soul. Psalm 94:19

Worry, anxiety, and fear are the same negative emotion they are just experienced on different levels. Similar to the rungs on a ladder. Imagine standing at a ladder and you take the step of worry, then step up to anxiety and the third step lands you at the top which is fear. Scripture commands us not to do any of these things; do not worry, do not be anxious and do not fear! God never commands us to do something that He has not equipped us to do. These negative emotions only exist when we give them room and feed them. Overcome these negative emotions by taking three steps in the opposite direction. First, know the source is the enemy who seeks to disrupt our peace. Wake up each morning prepared to strike down worry and do not give it room to grow. Turn every anxious thought into a prayer by transforming your worry list into a prayer list! Then take the final step and confess that Good is your loving Father and He cares for you! Start rejoicing and praising God for the conquering of the enemy. What worries you? Children, spouse, family, relationships, finance, employment, health? Write it down, pray, and release it to our Father in heaven and allow his will to be done on earth as it is in heaven and then rejoice in the victory in Jesus's name!

CAROLYN MACK

Carolyn Mack, Mother of 3, is a Social Worker who is passionate about helping people to reach their fullest potential. She enjoys spending time with her children, reading, writing, and doing all things crafty.

True Comforter

Peace I leave with you; my peace I give you. Not as the world gives.
Do not let your hearts be troubled and do not be afraid. John 14:27

Along a winding untraveled road, I cast my eyes upon great despair.

When the storms of life raging ever so near, I cherish those moments of calm.

Oh, how I have mourned the times that have passed by.

A time of triumph, a time of sadness, a time that is lost.

My heart grows lonely daily facing challenges that paralyze my soul.

Finding peace is what I seek.

God is my true comforter, yielding my all to Him. When I think of his graciousness, no longer will I suffer.

SHANTA' MACK

Shanta' Mack is a Mother, Veteran, Nurse, Event Planner, Author, and Educator. She is currently on the front lines of the Covid19 pandemic.

The Essence of Her

For you formed my inward parts; you knitted me together in my Mother's womb. I praise you, for I am fearfully and wonderfully made. Psalm 139:13

Stripped down to the very essence of her insecurities, she looked in the mirror. Within her, she held stories of pain, heartache, heartbreak, and of sickness and illness within the deepness of her eyes. Brown coco skin with butterfly blemishes, her nose is kissed with freckles. Her lips are puckered and she wears a natural smirk. Fine lines of aging adorn her face. Moving down her body and making her way to her bosom, she sighs at the once firm breasts that flowed with streams of life's sustenance. Her stomach is not flat and wears the stretch marks of four. Turning slightly to the left, her eyes followed the sway in her back that lead to her round backside. Her hips are wide, and her thighs are thick, perfect for the bearing of miracles. Her legs are strong with well-defined calves. She remembered the track star, cheerleader, and dancer she once was. Reminiscing of what was and embracing what is, she closed her eyes and inhaled deeply. With her head held high and her shoulders back, she opened her eyes and exhaled, stood firmly, and acknowledged all that is her truth. She is flawed yet flawless. Torn but not tattered. Beautifully broken but not in pieces. Down but not out. She is love. She is fire. She is strength, courage, joy, and pain. Predictably unpredictable. Perfectly imperfect. She has the soul of a warrior and the spirit of a butterfly. She is a survivor. She is greatness. She is a beautiful transformation in progress. She is enough. She is me.

SONYA Y. MAYERS

Sonya Mayers is a Registered Nurse, a Mother, and a missionary. She loves to volunteer and speak life to others. She can be found on social media FB, IG, Twitter as footstepsofanurse.

Simultaneous Joy

A time to weep, and a time to laugh, a time to mourn,
and a time to dance. Ecclesiastes 3:4

The outcome of grief is unique to one's personality, family dynamics, culture, religion, and health status. Thirty-two years after my husband died, I got the revelation that joy and weeping, mourning, and dancing are experienced together. Those dark moments [night] and joy [morning], were God-ordained companions. Instead of recognizing those moments, I had limited the river of joy by concentrating on enduring the journey and had adopted a "when this is over" mindset. When I finally chose to focus on the strength that came from joy and laughter without guilt, the memories of hugs, smiles, and encouragement from others, were transformed into joy coming at me in different forms. Each of them beautiful in their own way and just not temporary band-aids. I now know that joy is not limited to feelings or facial expressions. It is the ability to sleep, the support of family, friends, the gift of a clear mind, and being alive. Your night may be divorce, illness, or loss of a job, but know that you are in God's secret place where there are no limits to time or situations. You are in God's secret place where there are no limits to time or situations. Mourning decreases as the river of joy flows freely from a multifaceted God of love, increasing strength and laughter and removing guilt. We can smile at a photo, share jokes about a loved one, and use our night experiences to help someone else to realize that joy [morning] always comes in the morning; without fail.

DELICIA M. MAYES R.T.(R)(MR)

Delicia M. Mayes is a Radiologic and Magnetic Resonance Technologist, Author, Motivational Speaker, Prophetic Evangelist, Ministry Leader, and single Mother.

God's Real Name

Do not fear, for I am with you; do not be dismayed, for I am your God. I will strengthen you and help you; I will uphold you with my righteous right hand. Isaiah 41:10

In the middle of the night, at 3:00 am to be exact, I was awakened to missed calls and voicemails. I knew instantly that something was not right. My daughter and her 3 friends had been in a head-on car collision with a wrong-way drunk driver! As Christians, we are taught to be strong, pray, and trust God. I honestly allowed my emotions to take control of me by panicking and crying. During this emotional time, I heard a small voice say, "Go pray!" The Holy Spirit was telling me to talk to God, my comforter, strengthener, my daughter's protector, and healer. God's name is anything you need Him for at any time. He is always ready for any situation even when you are not because He loves you. I fell on my knees and shouted, "GOD! Save my only baby! Please send your angels to protect her and her friends. Lord, you said, "No weapon formed against us shall prosper". (Isaiah 54:17) I went to God 1st, spoke HIS word, trusted in Him, and let Him be in control. He showed me signs, wonders and miracles are real in today's world! Despite multiple fractures and surgeries my daughter and 1 friend survived! They both are totally healed and walking miracles! Believe in His word without a doubt and you WILL see His love! (Mark 11:22) What is God's name in your situation?

RUE MAYWEATHER

Rue Mayweather can still say after 30+ years that every parent should have a child-like her son. Rue is first and foremost a Christian, Mother, and MiMi.

Value Along the Journey

*Then shall He answer them saying, Verily I say
unto you, "In as much as ye did it not to one of the
least of these, Ye did it not to me." Matthew 25:45*

In our daily walk with God, every day will not be Sunday, but it can
be joyful; even on the darkest days when we feel that all hope is lost.
There are times when you need to allow your mind to rest and do not
think about anything or anyone. You may be wondering what this has
to do with value? I am so glad you asked! Value starts with self.
Value defines the importance of something or someone. Being able
to perceive value in someone else does not diminish your value
unless you allow it. When I talk to teens and adults in prison about
what led them to prison. I realize that it is possible for one to lose
their value. Values influence our attitudes and behaviors. People on
the streets who you see homeless were not always homeless. Their
current situation is not who they are. Everyone has value. Value is
like the pearl found at the depths of the sea. It is valuable and
priceless yet not visible. We have to search in each other and shout it
out with praise! "Sister, you look beautiful". "Brother, I love your
hair cut. Great! Congratulations! Keep reaching! Lastly, I'm praying
for you."

DYESHA MCCANTS

Dyesha McCants live in the Washington, DC metro area. She is the co-author of two children's books The Misadventures of Tarah and Darah: The Switch and The School Play. She is a 17-year veteran educator.

Gods Plan

For I know the plans I have for you," declares the Lord, "plans to prosper you and not to harm you, plans to give you hope and a future. Jeremiah 29:11

A few years ago, I was working at a job I did not like, working with people I did not like and not getting paid my worth, which I did not like! I was constantly in prayer and asking God, "What is my purpose? What do you want me to do?" Telling God, "I know you don't want me to keep doing something I am unhappy with. One morning, before school started, I was called into the principal's office. A complaint had been made against me and I was put on mandatory leave for at least six weeks. I was devastated! "God, where are you? How did this happen? This is not real!" One night while lying in my bed I could hear a faint whisper, "Book. Book. Book." So, the next morning I decided to sit down and write down one of the stories that my sister and I always tell people. This single-story turned into three. The time I was given to write down my stories was a blessing. I looked at it as something negative, but God had a plan for me. His plan was better than any thought or plan I could have imagined. During your time of uncertainty stop and listen to the quiet whisper of your soul. There is always a blessing wrapped up in the form of loss.

TRIESHA MCCANTS

Triesha McCants lives in the Washington, DC metro area. She is a 17-year veteran educator. She is the co-author of two children's books, *The Misadventures of Tarah and Darah: The Switch and The School Play.*

You Are in God's Thoughts

How precious also are Your thoughts to me, O God! How great is the sum of them! Psalms 139:17(NKJ)

GOD is always thinking about you, even when we are not thinking of ourselves and are at our lowest point. When we feel like we are unloved and unworthy to be loved, GOD has us in His thoughts and keeps us near to His heart. He knows what we need AND when we need it. He is considerate of what we experience and knows that we are hard-headed and willful. He NEVER turns his back on us, and we are NEVER out of his mind. He is with us ALWAYS. We let our minds wander and are distracted by our everyday lives. He knows that we are neglectful, but He does not hold that against us. He is faithful and ALWAYS thinking of us. He waits patiently for us to come to Him. We can only imagine the wonderful thoughts that He may have about us because He ONLY sees the good in us. We judge ourselves but God is NOT judgmental. He is LOVING, KIND, and our forever cheerleader. There are so many times that I thought I was forsaken by God, but He always showed me He was right there waiting for me to acknowledge him. He wants us to think of him just as much as He thinks of us!

APOSTLE GREG MCCURRY

Apostle Gregory McCurry is the founder of New Beginning Ministries Cleveland-based church. He longs to see lives transformed by introducing "A Real God, to Real People with Real Issues."

It Was Necessary

And we know that all things work together for good to those who love God, to those who are called according to His purpose.
Romans 8:28

We are assured that God is a partner in our labor. All things work together and are [fitting into a plan] for good to and for those who love God and are called according to [His] design and purpose. But as for you, you thought evil against me, but God meant it for Good. The first thing God said to tell you is, "QUIT TRIPPIN!" It ain't even about you, it is about GOD!! He said everything you been through, are going through, and will go through was necessary. It is just a moment in your momentum, but it was necessary. Your moment is what you are in, but not your expected end. Jeremiah 29:11 says God has an expected end. He knows the final outcome. We want the promise, but we do not want the process. The process is necessary before the promise, the steps are;

PROPHECY ~ PROCESS~ PROMISE

We got evicted from our church building, I got a divorce, and I lost my job. What I did not know was it was all working together for my good it pushed me into my DESTINY! Once I was able to receive God had a better life for me, I was able to purchase a better building, I married my helpmeet, and I was able to work for JESUS 24/7. I was finally able to understand that it was necessary! 2 Corinthians 4:17 says, *For this light affliction is preparing for us an **ETERNAL** weight of glory beyond all comparison.*

PASTOR TERESA S. MCCURRY

Pastor Teresa S. McCurry is an Author, Entrepreneur, and ordained minister of the Gospel of Jesus Christ. She co-labors with her husband, doing the work of the Lord as a ministry team.

Weeping May Endure

Weeping may endure for a night, but joy cometh
in the morning. Psalm 30:5

My daughter, Meesha Chanell Saxton, was born on October 17, 1995, with Sickle Cell Disease. Due to complications and the miseducation of this disease, she passed away on December 24, 1996. Even though my life was often violently tossed upon rough seas, I decided that my overall attitude would not become one of a victim, but of a victor. Knowing that Jesus was always somewhere on board helped me stay grounded. These scriptures became a reality in my life: *"Greater is He that is in you, than he that is in the world" (John 4:4)*. And *"Death and life are in the power of the tongue: and they that love it shall eat the fruit thereof." (Proverbs 18:2)*. I always believed that something GREAT would come out of her passing. I opened my salon and spa, Mimi's Hair Heaven & Spa, in her memory. It was more than a business; it was ministry. I made a lifelong decision to choose blessings and life. I chose to live life fully and abundantly. I have been a sickle cell advocate ever since. The Meesha Chanell Saxton (MCS ~ FUND) has a sole mission to generate unrestricted funds for Sickle Cell Anemia affected individuals. Through Supportive Services & Advocacy serving the needs of people plagued by this disease is not only a mission but a passion. This is my morning TIME!!

EVANGELIST MATTIE DANIELS MCNEAL

Evangelist Mattie Daniels McNeal is a licensed Minister and Registered Nurse. Her heart and anointing are to lead the lost, the lonely, and the hurting into a personal relationship with Jesus Christ.

From Grief to Grace

For by grace you are saved through faith. It is the gift of God. Ephesians 2:8

Whoever said nurses are not supposed to get involved in the lives of their patients has never been a nurse. We laugh, cry, and yes, grieve with our patients and their families.

One night on duty my patient was a man named Samuel who was HIV positive. As I went to the back medication room, the Lord said to me, "Samuel is your assignment tonight." I began to make excuses like Moses; I am too busy tonight. We don't proselytize at work." God reminded me of what I had promised Him when He asked in *Isaiah 6:8* "Who shall I send and who shall go? I said, "Here am I send me."

When I entered Samuel's room smiling, I introduced myself. His oxygen notable, his rib cage was protruding through his chest as he struggled to breathe. I noticed a Holy Bible on his table. He said his Aunt who was a Christian left it. He shared details about his life. He was not a Christian. As I held his hand, I told him about the unconditional love of Jesus Christ and how Christ demonstrated that love for everyone while we were still sinners (Romans 5:8). Then I asked him if he wanted to accept Christ into his heart and he said YES.

I came back two days later to check on Samuel, but he was not there. The nurses told me he had passed. I smiled, not about death, but about life. Samuel had gone from *grief to grace*. He closed his eyes on this side but when he lifted his eyes he was in the presence of God. (2nd Cor 5:8)

JOTWYLA MOORE

Jotwyla R. Moore is the Assistant Pastor of Restoring Life Ministries, the author of *The Encounter*, *A Certain Woman: Personal Application Guide to Living Life Without Doubts*, and *Devotions for the Seasoned Woman*. Mrs. Moore is an active blogger at Empowerment Encounters.

Life after Grief = RAISE

And after you have suffered a little while, the God of all grace, who has called you to His eternal glory in Christ, will himself restore, authorize, strengthen, and establish you. 1 Peter 5:10

We will all face heartache, discomfort, and sorrow as these things are an item on the buffet of life. There is no vaccination to immunize against it; therefore, none of us will escape this deep infliction. However, according to the scripture above, we have a promise that we can hold to as it tells us, ***Christ, will himself restore, authorize, strengthen, and establish you.*** Grief shows up at the door as an announcement that something attached to us has moved forward to the next life. Grief does not take "No" for an answer. We must let it in, but with the realization that it is <u>only</u> a visitor. There is no set duration for the stay. Grief has come to work, so allow it to labor in your presence. Just know that upon griefs departure comes a RAISE. The assurance of <u>R</u>estoration means we are more valuable than before the suffering. <u>A</u>uthorization empowers us to face hardships head-on as we have experienced and conquered in this area. God's grace provides <u>I</u>nitiative to begin again and renewed joy becomes the <u>S</u>trength we need to face tomorrow. <u>E</u>stablishment is provided to make what has been shaky in our lives firm again so that we can walk assuredly into our prearranged destiny.

R.C. NICHOLE

Richanda N. Birks, also known as R.C. Nichole, is a Sexual Trauma Survivor Advocate. She is a Minister, College Instructor, and Faith-based Workshop Facilitator.

<u>The Beauty of God</u>

*To give to them that mourn, beauty for ashes, the oil of joy
for mourning, the garment of praise for the spirit of
heaviness. Isaiah 61:3*

Have you ever asked yourself, "Where was God?" Have you ever wondered; where is this all-powerful, all-knowing, faithful, and loving God that exists? Those are valid questions to ask when you are being abused, mistreated, neglected, and abandoned. It is never in God's will for you to suffer. He has a plan for your life. He knows that we live in a fallen world and people have turned their backs on Him and everything that He represents. This, in turn, allows sin to take residence in the hearts and minds of the people. When traumatic incidents happen in your life, your soul is broken and pieces of yourself are damaged or lost. God desires to build a relationship with you so that he can heal you. He wants to take your broken pieces and put them back together so that you can be made whole. Life experiences can alter how we feel and what we think about ourselves. It is easy to forget what God says about us. We must remember to keep His word close to our hearts, speak His words from our mouths and He will give you peace and joy. God wants to love you past your pain.

Lord, when we are doubting your presence in our lives, help us remember the plans you have for us and your undying love.

TAMIKA L. PAIGE

Tamika Paige is a Wife, Mother, and advocate of love. She is 43 years young and happily married for 16 years with 2 young adult children. Her mission is to leave every person and place greater because she was there.

Scarred but Not Wounded

God is in the midst of her; she will not be moved. Psalms 46:5

Imagine at an early age all of your hopes and dreams being beaten out of you. Imagine a life where you never see anything positive for yourself, never being able to think beyond "today", merely praying just to get through the next 24 hours without being thrown down 14 stairs, burnt with an iron, knocked unconscious, taken from your home in a nightgown only to wake up with someone having sex with you. Well, this was life. My everyday life. No career goals, wedding visions, or plan of parenthood. Only meaningless apologies until the next time. I really do not recall how it ended, I wish I could say I became stronger and wiser, but I really do not know. Just one day we were over. As the years went on and I grew older, not seemingly affected by the trauma, moving carelessly through life, always putting love in the atmosphere, creating nurturing environments for those I love. I believe this was the cause of God turning my life around. It was not until I got saved and made changes in my thoughts and decisions that God blessed me with a husband, two beautiful and independent kids, and a career. The pain and hurt I have experienced in my early life are no comparison to how blessed I am now. Together my husband and I are a couple that has dedicated ourselves to each other in friendship, love, and business. We have created a foundation of foreverness with each other, with respect and accountability as our mission statement.

PRECIOUS SWAIN-PEAKS

Precious Swain is a Wife, Mother, Grandmother, and child of Yahuah. As a Pastor, Author, Life Coach, and Accountant her life is centered around empowering and motivating others.

The Joyous Ending

For I know את eth-the thoughts that I think toward you, says
YAHUAH, thoughts of peace, and not of evil, to give you an
expected end. YIRMEYAHU
(JEREMIAH) 29:11 את CEPHER

Throughout my journey, I have spent a lot of days wondering why.
Why did I have to go through the things that I went through? Not
really understanding why Yahusha bore the pain and suffering that
we may be redeemed by His blood. Like some people, I felt that I
was unworthy of being loved. I often wondered who could love this
broken battered little girl. Through time and trial, I have learned that
part of the reason we miss the joys of life is that we are focused on
the pain. It is time you recognize that the joy, happiness, and the
healing that we seek is already inside of us. Like a flower, we need to
take the time to water it daily. Each day we wake up we need to start
the day with praise. Why? Because we have the assurance of
knowing that when the praises go up the earth will experience
increase and ELOHIYM will bless us. *Psalms 67* allows us the time
to have a moment of peace. Peace and sleep are two totally different
things. Take time and remind yourself through reading, declaration,
meditation, or whatever works best for you of the promises of
Yahusha. Life is a gift; it is not something that we have earned. Nor
is it something that we are entitled to. So, let every day that you are
blessed with it be a day that you are happy simply to be alive.

PENEKALA "NEKA" PERKINS

Penekala "Neka" Perkins is a Senior Labor Relations Advisor with the Department of the Navy and a children's book co-author with her daughter, Faith.

Remain Faithful Amid Your Frustration

*And by faith, even Sarah, who was past childbearing age, was
enabled to bear children because she considered Him [God]
faithful who had made the promise.*
Hebrews 11:11

Often, when grieving, one does not know what to do more less how to feel. Traumatic experiences leave one with a sense of helplessness, hopelessness, and many times simply answerless. Many believers are taught to never question God; however, it is the weakened human flesh that becomes curious and simply wants to know, ''Why ME?'' All the while the real question is, ''Why not ME?'' It is in those moments of frustration that it seems almost impossible to find the next steps on the journey to grieve, to heal, and to find peace. The most important thing to remember during the darkest hour is that no matter what feeling is being experienced, remain faithful because God is just and fair. That is when you have to shift feelings of frustration to faith and believe that all things work together for good to those who love God and who are called according to his purpose. In May 2012, I lost my firstborn, Trinity. As frustrated as I would often become, I still remained faithful. I read God's word and focused on the promises He had already made. In our daily talks, I would tell him that He said, "To be fruitful and multiply" and that He also said, "He would give me the desires of my heart." As a result of my faith, in September 2013, I delivered a healthy baby girl who I named, Faith. No matter what it looks like, grieve, but remain faithful even in the midst of your frustrations.

SMONIQUE SMITH-PERSON

SMonique Smith-Person is most known for her work with *The Center for Missing and Exploited Children*. She also works to support organizations that reach out to children at risk of running away, abduction, or trafficking.

Why I Trust God So Much; JOY!!

Grace, mercy, and peace will be with us, from God the Father and
Jesus Christ, the Son of the Father, in truth and love.
2 John 1:3

I have a habit. It is an addiction called joy. Many times, people search for that "THING" in life that makes them feel whole. You know, things like passion, purpose, talents, and gifts. Often, it is something that stands out boldly. It is an easy identifier that people will come to know you by. It may even be seen as your personal power. In 1968, I was abducted as a baby and raised by a manipulative and very abusive individual. I was sheltered enduring unimaginable torture for decades without an identity. My childhood was beyond bleak, to say the least. How could a child surface successfully without proper rearing of emotional, social, physical, and intellectual development? I escaped because I knew that there was joy out in the world and that He would get me through. Insert God's gift, my addition; His grace, and mercy. He instilled in me sheer Joy and the ability to seek it. I made it a habit to find joy during my journey every single day. In doing so, ultimately, I discovered this path was my assignment. Acknowledging and accepting that made me fill that void of feeling whole. Noting, I was free long before I knew it. That type of faith had me taking advantage of all the opportunities the world has to offer. After 20 years of searching for my true identity after being what most would call a *"Missing Milk Carton Kid."* I am one of 7 surviving sisters that each is over the age of 50, BUT GOD!

CELESTE PINCKNEY

Celeste Pinckney is a native of Baltimore, MD. She is a Mother, Grandmother, Daughter, and Sister. It has been her mission to care for, offer hope, and spread inspiration to those in need. She retired from the Federal Government in 2014 and is now a Certified Grief Coach.

A Navigational GPS to Get Through Grief

This is what the LORD says, "Stand at the crossroads and look; ask for the ancient paths, ask where the good way is, and walk in it, and you will find rest for your souls." But you said, "We will not walk in it." Jeremiah 6:16

Three things will guide you through grief;

God, People, and Scripture lead you to its defeat.

Separating yourself from all three at this time,

will make joy in the journey much harder to find.

God comes first, His ways are higher than ours.

His Son Jesus Christ knows all about scars.

Jesus experienced grief when He felt alone on the cross.

People are important for support and advice.

Realize they want what is best for you and are just being nice.

Family and friends, sisters and brothers in Christ,

Everyone's grief is different, we have all lived different lives.

Scripture is always a source of reflection,

There are so many verses in God's word that deserve closer inspection.

AMANDA RANDOLPH

Amanda Randolph is a devoted Wife, Mother, and retired US Army veteran. She loves God and sharing her faith journey with others.

<u>Goodness of God</u>

*I remain confident of this: I will see the goodness of the LORD
in the land of the living. Wait for the LORD; be strong and
take heart and wait for the LORD.*
Psalm 27:13

Say to yourself "God is still good." You may think that it is impossible to feel anything other than pain as you are grieving the loss of a loved one. That may be true because, at that moment, pain overshadows everything else. But in the midst of your pain, you still have a testimony. You may even ask yourself "What is there to testify about?" Even in the midst of the pain, hurt, sadness, and loss. you can still testify to the goodness of God. David declares in Psalm 27:13 that he is confident he will see the goodness of God in the land of the living. I believe David was encouraging himself as he came to the end of his own resources and remembered all the time's God protected, covered, and delivered him. We often like to quote, "O taste and see that the Lord is good." We forget the preceding verse, verse 6, in which a poor man cried out and the Lord heard him. It does not matter what caused the man to cry out to the Lord, I just know that he did, and God heard. Knowing God hears the cry of my heart encourages me to call on Him. When I do, I have this confident assurance that He will come to my aid. You too can say with surety the Lord Is good. Both you and I can trust Him. Your testimony of God's goodness not only encourages you but has the power to help someone else.

THADDEUS Y. RANDOLPH

Thaddeus Randolph is a dedicated Husband and Father. He is an Army veteran of 21 years. He is passionate about preaching, coaching, counseling.

The God of the Hills and Valleys

*There is a time for everything, and a season for every
activity under the heavens: a time to be born and a time to
die. Ecclesiastes 3: 1-8*

In life we all experience seasons of highs and lows, hills, and valleys. Ecclesiastes 3:1-8 speaks of the different seasons we encounter in life. There are twenty-eight seasons recorded in those verses that are symbolic of the emotional and physical expressions we each may experience. It is encouraging and comforting to know regardless of the season or time we find ourselves in, we can find victory because He is the God of the hills and valleys! The advisors to the king of Syria reduced God to a one-trick pony, by suggesting that His strength was only in the hills or mountains, and not the plains and valleys. In other words, the people of God can only experience success in the hills because they have the tactical advantage. Unfortunately, some people of faith have the same mindset. A mountaintop experience means God is with me, while a valley experience means I have been forsaken. Do not get it twisted and think that if things are going good in life, it is from God and if things are going bad, it is must be from the devil. This mindset implies success equals blessings and favor, while failure means God disapproves, is disinterested, or is displeased. Like the advisors to the king of Syria, we must be careful not to fall into the trap of putting God in a spiritual box. God assures the believer that He will never leave or forsake you. You can always trust God no matter the season to keep his word!

PETRICE M. MCKEY-REESE

Petrice M. McKey-Reese is a Mother, Wife, Grandmother, and child of God. She is a retired Veteran and loves helping people.

Living A New Normal

My flesh and my heart faileth: but God is the strength of my heart and my portion forever. Psalm 73:26

When my Mother passed away, unexpectedly, a little over two years ago my world rocked. My Mother was always my biggest supporter and my rock! My life went into a downward spiral for about eight months and I could not come out of it. I was thankful to God for so many things surrounding her death; I had just spent a week at home with her, she laid down and went to sleep and did not suffer, my sister found her and not my niece. Although my life seemed to be spiraling out of control, I knew God was hearing my cries and prayers. My faith never wavered! One day I cried like I had never cried since the passing of my Mother. I cannot remember how long I cried, all I know is that when the crying was finished a freshness came. It was like I was renewed. I knew that God had given me what I needed to start learning to live a new normal. That is what my days are like living without my Mother. That cry was what God gave me for me to start living again. I had to figure out how I was going to live a new normal without my rock. Losing a parent is hard for any child but I believe when it is unexpected it is worse. When you have a close relationship with that parent, as I did, you have a void that will never be filled. Amid the pain, you must find a way to move on. I cherish and celebrate those things we shared together. I do not let anyone tell me that I should not still be crying. I cry when I need to, I talk to her when I want to, and I go sit at her graveside for visits. God helped me to get through it all. He knew how much time I would need and just what to do to set me on the path to recovery. God is all-knowing and is great. I always knew He would see me through. I just had to hold on. You can have peace and healing too. Hold on.

ALICIA RODMAN

Alicia Rodman of AliciaCoaches.com specializes in Coaching and Motivational Speaking. She partners with beautiful, smart, successful women to move them to their next level.

<u>Rediscovering Joy</u>

The thief does not come except to steal, kill, and to destroy. I have come that they may have life and that they may have it more abundantly. John 10:10

We laughed and laughed, just like old times as we reminisced about being kids and talked about life. Somehow it always led back to laughing; we just could not help it! Two days later, while sleeping on his hospice bed upon which he laughed, my closest cousin slipped into eternity. We were supposed to grow old together. Always living, loving, and laughing but that dream was forever lost in an instant. I was here with lots of family members for support, but I still felt alone. How would I go on without my cousin, William? How do you get abundant life after a loss and live through the pain? Simply put, choose life over and over again. Living is more than breathing. Living is what keeps your spirit alive. It connects you to those you love. After losing my cousin, I kept thinking that my "dance partner" was gone. Eventually, I had to move through it to get back to what it was I had always felt about him anyway, I loved him. The pain that comes from the loss of the person not being there is bad enough. You finally realize the absence of the love you received from them is what hurts the most. Close your eyes, do you remember how that emotion felt? Was it love, joy, peace, or something else? Feel it in your body. Take time to extract that feeling, hold it close. Choose to live abundantly, every day. Consider how your abundant living makes you feel. It makes you think, speak, and act differently. Now, I dance harder than I ever danced before because I have chosen to feel and embody the joy and love in my cousin's life into my own compounded with that which is already inside of me. Say this *with* me: "Today, I choose to live abundantly."

PATRICIA ROGERS

Patricia Rogers is a Business Coach, Event Coordinator, and Multilevel Marketer. Pat hosts annual networking events for entrepreneurs to connect and build their professional networks while achieving wealth.

A Butterfly's Encouragement

I met with a joyful butterfly, although I cannot recall his name, he is colorful and enthusiastic as he began to float my way.

He said, "I'm searching for my mate and pretty soon I will find her, but I wanted to pay you a visit and give you this friendly reminder."

Everyone would like to fly, radiate, and cheerfully sing but each of these is the result of overcoming adversities.

Every caterpillar has a cocoon where she is forced to face herself that is where we develop the strength to advance to higher steps.

Your struggles are not to harm you but to build you up inside so that you would have the strength to soar like butterflies."

Affirmation:

With every success comes challenges and hard work, but when you face each difficulty and overcome them, they should move you into a space that inspires you to achieve even more success. **~Patricia Rogers~**

Prayer:

Father, thank you for another day which I did not have to see. When I start each day, I know not what it will bring, but prepare me so that I can face each challenge. Please show me what your will is so that I can be an inspiration to those I will serve.

DOROTHY MAY ROSS

Dorothy Ross is a Women's Midlife and Beyond Empowerment Coach, CEO at Women Rocking Life, and Co-Author of Bouncing Back in Thriving Times.

As Close as a Sister

Two people can resist an attack that would defeat one person alone.
A rope made of three cords is hard to break. Ecclesiastes 4:12 GNT

I am the oldest of three sisters. We all had families and we started going in different directions. We talked to each other, but we were not close nor did we come together as a family,

I received the call at work that if I wanted to see my baby sister alive, I needed to get to the hospital. She had a heart attack and did not make it. I felt lost, guilty, and hurt. I could have done more to interact and stay close. Two weeks before, both sisters dropped by the house and we laughed and talked and had a ball.

My middle sister not long after had a stroke and had to go into a nursing home. I began to feel the loss. Working every day, taking care of my family, and visiting my sister was taking a toll on me. I needed time away to refresh and refuel or my health would be in trouble too.

I attended a conference in Phoenix and met two women on the last day of the conference. We exchanged numbers. They both let me know they wanted to be friends and now we are still best friends after twelve years.

I am not trying to replace my own sisters. I believed in prayer and God replaced my loss, allowing me to have friends when I needed them, just like a sister. When I got the call saying I had breast cancer both Dawn and Arlene were there. They were my prayer partners and my encouragement.

NADIA SANGUINETTI

Nadia Sanguinetti is a Certified Professional Coach, (CPC). Owner of ***Nadia Speaks, Nadia Coaches, Nadia Inspires***; a Personal Development Coaching designed to provide personal development coaching, tools, and resources for women.

Finding My Way Back to Me!

Trust in the LORD with all your heart and do not lean on your own understanding. In all your ways acknowledge Him, And He will make your paths straight. Proverbs 3:5-6

If we are completely honest with ourselves we can say that at some point and time we all have experienced something in life that has left you devastated so much that we feel like the wind has been knocked out of us, made you forget your name, and everything else about you. Leaving you to wonder, how do I get back to me? How do I find ME again? The journey is the journey and the process is the process. If you are willing to put your trust in God and let Him light the path you will discover both joy and peace along the journey, AND joy in the journey of finding your way back to YOU! The challenge for some people when they encounter a hiccup in life is, they begin to question, "How do I go on from here? A better question is, "How do I grow from here?" What can I harvest from this experience to create a better me? How do I navigate this change in my life without carrying a burden? Be determined to live and find your way back to you. Do this by understanding that life is full of cycles and the strongest people understand that fact. They take every opportunity to learn, grow, and develop from every experience. There are beautiful gems all around you guiding your path, each with a lesson, a truth, or a bit of wisdom to carry you to the next place on your journey. Finding your way back simply means there is a you that is waiting to be discovered. A *YOU* that you never knew existed. Someone who is embracing all life has to offer. No longer necessary to compete with anyone else. Strong enough to look in the mirror and recognize the power, grace, and strength that allows you to be authentic in the pursuit of your life's purpose no matter what!

SADIJA A. SMILEY

A certified grief recovery specialist, Sadija is the founder of Stillborn and Infant Loss Support- SAILS. She is the Mother of three beautiful daughters, two on earth and one in heaven.

Joy from the Community

Encourage one another and build each other up.
1 Thess 5:11

This verse suggests that we motivate and encourage one another. Do not be discouraged on this journey of grief, let us remind one another that better days lie ahead. We are in this together. Having a community around us reminds us that we are not fighting our battles alone. Community is where we find comfort in difficult times. We can continually remind each other of where our joy comes from. Community is essential on our journey. Your community may consist of your friends, classmates, family, church members, and/or coworkers. Allow them to rally around you, praying with and for you. Even when life seems too overbearing and you feel like giving up, your community will be that breath of fresh air, the hand that brushes the dirt off of your shoulders, and the smile to keep you going.

My Prayer: Heavenly Father, what a wonderful message contained in this beautiful verse of scripture. Thank you for reminding us of the importance of community. That we should encourage and uplift each other. Thank you for reminding us that we are members of Your community and we are not alone. As we travel on this journey of grief, Father, let us find joy in our community and in the journey. I pray that we are reminded that joy is not necessarily the absence of suffering, but the presence of God. Help me to share this message of comfort and joy with others, for Your greater glory, in Jesus's name I pray, AMEN.

KEEBA SMITH

Keeba Smith is a Wife and Mother. She is a Biology Teacher working on her Doctorate and U.S. Army Veteran. She is the published Author of "Trust God! From a Mother's Grief to Affirming Faith; How God Gives Us Twice as Much.

Speaking Prosperity in Your Life

"For I know the plans I have for you," declares the Lord, plans to prosper you and not to harm you, plans to give you hope and a future." Jeremiah 29:11

Are you trusting God's plan for your life? Are you letting His will be done in your life? Many times, we forget that God is in control of all things. The challenges and struggles we face in life are all a part of God's plans. Romans 8:28 (NIV), *"And we know that in all things God works for the good of those who love Him, who have been called according to His purpose."* While things happen that may not FEEL good, trust that God is working it out FOR your good. We must speak prosperity into our lives and know that it is all according to His plan. We are destined for greatness. While this journey called life will have its ups and down, never lose faith in God. He knows what is best for us.

"The will of God will never take you, where the grace of God will not protect you."

TRUST GOD!

TAKIA CHASE SMITH

Takia Smith is a Wife and Mother. She is a licensed Cosmetologist and U.S. Army Veteran. She is a Best-Selling Author. She is currently pursuing certification as a Massage Therapist.

Do Not Complain, Always Stay Positive

And the children of Israel complained against Moses and Aaron: and the whole congregation said to them, "If only we had died in the land of Egypt!" Numbers 14:2

What is your first instinct when something bad happens to you, what first comes to your head? Do you complain or grumble or do you say, "I know all is well"? For the children of Israel, their first line of action was always to complain and grumble against God and their leaders. God had intentionally taken the children of Israel through the wilderness in order to give them certain experiences they needed for their journeys ahead. The children of Israel needed to learn positively from the wilderness experience. But the reverse was the case; they allowed it to impact their lives negatively by complaining, grumbling, and being negative about every hardship they faced. What are you struggling with today? What troubles you? What have you lost? Whatever it is, know this. While the situation may be bad, God can make something good come out of it. If only we maintain a positive attitude and avoid complaining and grumbling like the children of Israel did. **Prayer:** LORD God, please help me to stay positive always, never to speak with my tongue anything that will annoy you, but to always speak in faith know that you are in control.

THERESA (TRE') SMITH

Theresa (Tre') Smith is a Wife, Step-Mother, Grandmother, and Child of God. She is an Army Veteran. She specializes in executive leadership, mentorship, and community service.

Jesus Joy

God is our refuge and strength; a very present help in trouble.
Therefore, we will not fear though the earth gives way, though the
mountains be moved into the heart of the sea, though its waters
roar and foam, though the mountains tremble at its swelling.

Psalm 46: 1-3

For many years after a traumatic experience, I lived in the shadows of God. I always believed in God but felt He was not within me. My entire life, I have worked to give back in any way possible – yet my heart never felt Jesus Joy. Whenever possible I would provide for the less fortunate, assisted in the enhancement of schools and education, beautify the community, or donate to a cause. It was not until I rededicated my life to God that I was able to experience Jesus Joy. My experience is beyond words. I still experience trials, tribulations, sorrow, disappointments, fear, despair, and depression. However, knowing that I am not experiencing any of these things alone, makes them bearable. Jesus Joy is not an emotion that can be forced, fabricated, or replicated. My prayer for whoever is reading this is that you will experience Jesus Joy in your own heart. Joy comes when we spend our life praising God.

VALERIE STANCILL

Valerie Stancill is the founder of *Cloud 9 Wellness Healing Center.* She is a licensed massage therapist, certified holistic wellness coach, Domestic Violence Advocate, Yoni/Reiki practitioner, Author, speaker, founder of Authentic YOU, and Movement and Purpose to Wellness radio show host.

Plan for Purpose

For I know the thoughts and plans that I have for you, says the Lord, thoughts, and plans for welfare of peace and not for evil, to give you hope in your outcome. Jeremiah 29:11

Life has been known to be rude and disrespectful. This scripture has been something I have coined as a reminder, that no matter what, there is purpose in everything that happens in our lives. You may not be able to comprehend it while you are going through it. You may find yourself questioning God. His plan is to take us to a glorious future but not without the growth that comes from persevering through trials and tribulations. When we learn perseverance, we will learn joy and peace. He may decide that you have to stay right where you are for a minute so that you understand His plan to prosper you. Some journeys are not easy and may take years to see and understand your whys. When you understand that the perseverance was for a purpose, it is that purpose which takes you to an expected end. God wants you to know in this journey of pain, heartache, and trauma, He has a plan. Even when you cannot see or comprehend or understand, God still has a plan. Do you keep asking God, why? You can wallow in self-pity or decide to allow this to be a way to discover your purpose. Choose to accept it knowing there is a greater purpose for your life. Your test will be a testimony, your pain has been for His gain. Understand there is purpose in your pain. It is reassuring because it means God will grace us with success and blessings in our lives, it is reassuring because it means God has a purpose for our pain and suffering. What hard thing are you going through? He will give you hope in the midst of it.

YOLONDA MICHELLE NELSON-SWAIN

Yolonda provides support to survivors of homicide who are experiencing grief. She provides them with tools for healthy coping and strengthening their relationships as they embark on the process of healing. She is a Wife and Mother.

Overcoming Sadness

The Lord is close to the brokenhearted, and he saves those whose spirits have been crushed. Psalm 14:18

As we navigate through life, it becomes apparent that we cannot appreciate happiness without experiencing sadness. Every one of us will experience sadness in our lives. As babies, we become sad when our caregivers take away our favorite toy. As teens, we may become sad if we are not accepted by a certain group. Adults might experience sadness when children leave home. Whatever it may have been, we have all experienced sadness. At that moment we thought we would never get past it, but somehow, we did. We were able to find happiness in other places; making friends with someone else or finding out who we were after the children left the nest. Losing a loved one, without a doubt can be crushing. Knowing that we will not hear their voice or see them smile can be heartbreaking and difficult to bear. Although the loss of a loved one does not compare to losing a job or being rejected, we may feel as if we will never get past the loss or get over the sadness, but we can. How do you ask? Allow yourself to feel the pain and grieve your loss. You do not have to be "strong" for everyone else. Write down your feelings – the good, the bad, and the ugly. Seek out your purpose after the loss and most importantly, remember that God is there and that you can still find joy in the journey.

TERRIE A. SYLVESTER

Prophetess Terrie Ann Sylvester is Sr Project Coordinator and is a volunteer Zumba Instructor. She values family and the cultivation of relationships.

Goodbye Grief

Finally, brethren, whatever things are true, whatever things are noble, whatever things are just, whatever things are pure, whatever things are lovely, whatever things are of good report, if there is any virtue and if there is anything praiseworthy—meditate on these things. The things you learned, received, heard, and saw in me, these do, and the God of peace will be with you. Philippians 4:8

Out of all the situations and circumstances in the world, you had to walk into mine. You came in like a bully invading my thoughts and emotions. You demanded my attention day and night. You were relentless, unwilling to loosen your hold. I pushed you away but in your pursuit of domination, you wiggled your way back into my presence, robbing me of my peace. In the past, I would let you win every time; allowing you to strengthen your hold on my heart and mind. Today I serve you notice. I will not be a participant in your quest for domination. I will not think about you. I will not allow you to bully me with thoughts of what could have been. Thoughts of what has been lost. Thoughts of what is now gone forever. This is what I intend to do. You really need to catch a clue. Goodbye grief, you cannot have my peace. My thoughts are no longer with you.

EVANGELIST MARIA TERRY

Evangelist Terry is a best-selling author, preacher, mentor, and motivational speaker who addresses critical issues affecting an individual's social and spiritual development. She is the founder of an outreach non-profit organization Healed and Whole Ministries along with early mornings via Facebook live; The Bounce Back.

Mountain Mover

If ye have faith as a grain of mustard seed, ye shall say unto this mountain, "Remove hence to yonder place," and it shall remove, and nothing shall be impossible unto you. Matthew 17:20

Rarely does one reflect and examine themselves to question their own faith. We often have many opinions regarding others and their beliefs. Today, ask yourself, "How big is my faith?" Do I have the faith that kicks around pebbles or am I a mountain mover? A pebble pusher is one who complains, while mountain movers praise. Pebble pushers kick around small imaginary wishes, while a mountain mover dreams big uncomprehensive ideas that only can be done with God. Pebble pushers doubt and blame others for their situation. Mountain movers believe even when they cannot see, feel, or hear God. They know it is not how you feel it is what you know. Mountain movers know that no weapon formed against them will ever prosper (Is.54:17) Mountain movers are active because they know that faith without works is dead (James2:17) Pebble pushers wait and wish. Mountain movers praise and worship, they pray and keep praying because they know that prayer still works. Today tell yourself, I am moving mountains in my life not because I think I can but because with Christ all things are possible, and I know I can.

MINISTER CARRIE THOMAS

Meet Minister Carrie Thomas who is an Author, a prolific speaker, life coach, and minister of the gospel of Jesus Christ. Carrie is the proud founder of Ministry Without Walls/MEMFTH Outreach in Clinton, Maryland.

Centerpiece

Be still and know that I am God! Psalm 46:10

Start your day by giving God the first 15 minutes. In doing this, seeking first the kingdom of God and His righteousness, more than you could ever think or imagine will be yours. (paraphrasing Matthew 6:33)

Today's devotional pricked my heart in such a way that I had to share. We are all guilty of this, including me, placing other things as the center of our joy instead of God, our Creator, and the One Who makes life possible for us.

Re-centering our lives around a relationship with God is a process in which God has total patience and grace. He knows that you will only center your life around that which you chiefly enjoy. He knows it takes time for Him to become the chief of your joy. This is most definitely the highest, most important process you can pursue.

When He becomes your chief, the center, of your joy, all other aspects of life find their proper place. When He becomes your chief joy, your emotions will no longer be subject to the fickle, fleeting things of the world, but rather grounded in the unshakeable, unchanging nature of your heavenly Father.

May you offer your whole heart to God today that you might fully enjoy Him. May His love and presence be the foundation of your life. And may you seek a relationship with Him above all else.

ANGELA B. THOMPSON

Angela Thompson is an Expressive Writing Coach and Journal Enthusiast. She enjoys helping others find the gift of their voice in storytelling.

My Resting Joy

"May the God of hope fill you with all joy and peace as you trust in him, so that you may overflow with hope by the power of the Holy Spirit." Romans 15:13

Your life may take you down many roads with various twists, turns, and dead ends, but the journey is what enriches your soul. You learn your lessons and earn your blessings. You may lose some things but gain other things. Through it all, your path is yours to travel, but the joy in your journey comes from knowing God has already ordered your steps. Along the way, we may forget to tap into our reserves when we need rest and re-fuel our lives. Take a moment. Breathe. Pullover to your spiritual rest stop and fill up your tank with some sustenance. Be sure to run it over with the joy and peace of God and experience the richness of your life while you are *finding joy in the journey.* When life overtakes me, I take pause and rest. The fullness submerges me into its vastness. Hopeful of the comfort, support, and shelter blanketing and engulfing me by its warmth. It is familiar, yet beyond my understanding. Embracing me with the surplus of hope. Standing in the gap of my faithfulness, I can rest my body, mind, and spirit. With an all-encompassing peace, succumbing to all its fullness, humbled by the intensity. I refuel my resting joy.

EVANGELIST TANYA R. THOMPSON

Evangelist Tanya R. Thompson is a Mother, Nurse, best-selling Author, speaker, and CEO of Glory After the Rain Ministries. She hosts an early morning devotional show that can be found on Facebook and YouTube.

Trust and Believe

So, shall they fear the name of the LORD from the west and his glory from the rising of the sun? When the enemy shall come in like a flood, the Spirit of the LORD shall lift a standard against him. Isaiah 59:19

In each one of our lives, a little rain must fall. This rain may be equivalent to grievous circumstances and diverse temptations, or it may simply be a battle that rages from within. There will be times that we may be able to hear the Lord loud and clear. Then, there will inevitably be other times when it feels that you have been ostracized to a time and place where you feel as if God has completely left you. There may even be times when you ask God questions concerning your current state of affairs. When rain falls, we run for a covering. We may stand under umbrellas. We may pray and wait out the storm. Sometimes, we even stand still and wait for the storm to pass before we move forward. There are times when the rain around us becomes dangerous and we are instructed to take cover. We are instructed that it may be treacherous if we attempt to maneuver a storm of a certain degree. It may be tumultuous all around. But I always find comfort in anticipating the beauty that comes following a storm. There may be debris that was left in the middle of our path. In this instance, we may be forced to choose a different route to the same destination. It may be uncomfortable, but the journey is necessary. It may take a little longer than originally anticipated but it is reachable. We are free to safely move towards our destiny and complete our intended journey, after the rain. Trust and believe that God will do what He promised. While on the journey, hold fast to His unchanging hand.

SHAWNTIA THORPE

Shawntia Thorpe, a native of Greensboro NC, is a Mother, with a loving son name Tre. She is an Assistant Manager.

Believe in God's Eternal Promise of Heaven

But lay up for yourselves treasures in heaven, where neither moth
nor rust destroys and where thieves do not break in and steal.
Matthew 6:20

Consider for a second, the possibility that there is a place we all go to after we have died. Consider for a second that all your loved ones who have passed have gone to be with the Lord. The reality of the scripture that Heaven is real! I mean we know there is a God, we know there is more to life than what we see, and as believers, we have seen God's words in action in our lives, family, and society. If we can believe that Jesus saves, that Jesus heals, that he delivers, he protects, then we must also believe what he says, when He said, *"In my Father's house there are many mansions there."* God's got something great prepared for us after this life. The implication of this is that this world is not the end. We will meet our loved ones we have lost, and we will be in paradise at the end of our pilgrimage here on earth.

Prayer: Father God, please give me the grace to know that my loved ones that passed are at home with you, keep me prepared for you always, and all I need to make it to your glorious kingdom please grant unto me in Jesus name.

BRENDA TORAIN

Brenda Torain is the CEO and Director of 2 Nursing Care facilities that provide housing for seniors and adults with developmental and memory issues. She is skilled in providing quality care so her residents can age in peace.

Leave the Past Where it Belongs

But one thing I do, forgetting those things which are behind, and reaching forth unto those things which are before. Philippians 3:13

2 Corinthians 5:17 reads, *Therefore if anyone is in Christ, he is a new creation; old things have passed away; behold, all things are become new.* This means the moment you give your life to Christ, you are no longer accountable for your past sinful actions. The blood of Jesus wipes that record and gives you a new beginning and fresh start. That means to really grow and succeed as a Christian you must forget your sins of before and focus on who you are in Christ. In the reference scripture above, Paul the apostle emphasized that he did not live in the past but was always focused on the future. Even as a believer if he made a mistake yesterday, he left that mistake in yesterday and moved on to the new day, a free man. We must not allow ourselves to be burdened and bound by events of the past. You must move on, and you must move on now! If not, the beautiful future God is planning for you will be wasted. David moved on after he lost his first son with Bathsheba (2 Samuel 12:16-25), soon he had Solomon who later became king (1 Kings 1: 38-40). For Lot, the death of his wife did not mark his end He moved on (Genesis 19:26,30). The prophet Ezekiel also lost his wife. That did not stop him from serving God or prophesying on the streets of Jerusalem (Ezekiel 24:15-18). You too must move on from the past and run towards your future.

Prayer: Holy Father, like Paul the apostle, the wisdom and courage to leave the past behind, and pursue my future please grant unto me in Jesus' name.

BETTY J. TYLER

Betty is a native of Prince George's County, MD, Mother of 2, IT professional for the Federal Government, freelance blogger, and Author. At her local church, she works with the children's ministry and is a civic leader in her community.

The Measure of a Father

"And I will be a Father to you, and you shall be sons and daughters to me", says the Lord almighty.
2 Corinthians 6:18

I had just ended the year with some obstacles and personal challenges. During that time of turmoil, it would have been comforting to have a loving Father, a strong side, an arm of protection. The word Father has always been an uncomfortable word for me to embrace. When I hear the word Father, I do not recall any memories, nor can I put a face or smell to the word. I do not know a voice to associate with the word Father. Our heavenly Father, God, is always spoken about in church. I knew who God was, but what is a Father? As I examined the word, I got clarity that a Father is someone that contributes to the production & development of another being. He has a social relationship or bond with his offspring. He teaches, provides, uplifts, leads, and his presence is felt and known. Furthermore, He leaves an inheritance for his children. One day while in meditation, I stumbled upon the following scripture. *The Spirit Himself testifies with our spirit that we are God's children. Now if we are his children, then we are heirs--heirs of God and co-heirs with Christ; If so be that we suffer with Him, that we may be also glorified together. Romans 8: 16 – 17.* The more I read this passage; it spoke to me loud and clear. I am the daughter of the most-high God. You may be without a natural Father, but you have a heavenly Father that has left an inheritance for you. He will fill all voids and take away the hurt. He will replace it with joy and His immeasurable love.

LISA DOVE WASHINGTON

Media Entrepreneur is a great way to describe Lisa Dove Washington. As the CEO of her own magazine, publishing company, Author, and Radio Co-host, this Washington DC native is making her mark on the work through her words and writing.

Look Above

Set your minds on things that are above, not on things that are on earth. – Colossians 3:2 ESV

So many times, I can remember fussing about the same things continuously. I was repeating the same complaints, exerting the same negative energy, and running the same frustrating events and scenarios over and over again in my head. I could not seem to shake the feeling to express my hurt, anger, and frustration about things that were going on in my life that for the most part, I could NOT control. I felt mistreated and disrespected and the need to share that was unyielding. I sounded much like that record that used to spin on the record player that got stuck in a groove and played the same chorus or verse over and over again. That sounds like it would drive you crazy right? You could not wait to move the needle and push it forward to get to the rest of the song.

My Mother used to tell me all the time to stop focusing on those things that I cannot control and to put my efforts into those things I can control. More often than not, the thing I could control was ME.

In Philippians 1:22-25, Paul was an old man when he was in prison in Rome awaiting execution, everything was taken away from him, but there was one thing they could not take away from him: his purpose. But Paul chose to stay focused on his purpose, even when he lost everything, he had everything. He was purposed to serve God by serving others.

Let your eyes look directly forward, and your gaze be straight before you – Proverbs 4:25 ESV

DEANNA WILLIAMS

DeAnna Wallace-Williams is a devoted servant of God, theology major, Co-Author, Youth and Adult Bible Teacher, Entrepreneur. Deanna has a heart to be committed to serving God's people.

What Shall I Do?

Now unto Him, that is able to do exceedingly, abundantly, above all that we ask or think, according to the power that worketh in us. Ephesians 3:20

When we set our thoughts unto God and His wondrous promises, there is nothing to worry about. No matter the dilemma, obstacle, or pain that attempts to block our path, God has the power to work it out. Even when we think we have devised the perfect plan of escape, God's Word tells us that He can do more than we could ever imagine with our limited capacities and abilities. Sometimes the weight of not knowing how a situation will turn out is unbearable. *Ephesians 3:20* reminds us that God is the Source. We must believe in God's omnipotence, omnipresence, and His omniscience. God knows the beginning and the end. God goes before us in every situation. Nothing catches God by surprise. He never slacks on his job. God is not like us, He does not clock-in late for work or call-off sick. He does not daydream or play games on His mobile devices while we sit in perilous anguish. God sees all and knows all. The best laid out plan by mere humans fails miserably in comparison to God's abundance. To exceed our ways is an amazing thought, and God adds abundantly. That alone is more than we could ever aspire to. He turns it up even more and adds above. There are three superlatives to describe God's abilities. His ways always outsmart and outweigh our mere humanness. Rest in the Word of God. When weariness sets in, think your best thought. Be assured that God has a plan that we could never even imagine.

BELINDA WILEY

Belinda is a Wife, Mother, Grandmother, and avid book lover.

All Things on Earth are Transient

And he thought to himself, saying, "What shall I do since I have no room to store my crops?" So, he said, "I will do this: I will pull down my barns and build greater and there I will store all my crops and goods." And I will say to my soul, "Soul, you have many years; take your ease; eat, drink, and be merry." But God said to him, "Fool! This night your soul will be required of you; then whose will those things be which you have provided.
Luke 12:17-20

The parable told by Jesus is consistent with what the majority of us are trying to achieve today, which is not bad, except that most times we tend to take it too far. That is financial security. Every one of us wants to get to a point where we do not have to work or struggle. A point where we have a steady stream of income from different directions. A point where we just relax on an island or holiday resort somewhere and the money keeps rolling in non-stop. Guess what, I am working towards that too, and I guess that is what the rich man in the scripture achieved and then he said now I can rest and enjoy. However, God had something else to say. What does this teach us? It teaches us that wealth and money should not come before our relationship with God or our wellbeing. Have you lost some money? Have you ever lost a business deal? Has something gone wrong in your financials? If yes, thank God for life, and then decide to learn from it. Contemplate where and how you got it wrong and do it again. The most important thing is you still have your life, and that means there is the chance that you will get it right this time.

Prayer: Lord Jesus, help my focus to be on you, no matter what. Help me to always put you and your kingdom first.

JOAN THOMPSON WILSON

Joan Wilson is a Business Strategist, Speaker, Author, and Content Champion. She coaches people to champion their dreams, businesses, and revenue goals.

I Am a Champion

Yes, pursue them, for you will surely
overtake them and without fail recover all.
Psalm 30:5

Oftentimes in life, you look up and say to yourself, "How did I get here?" It is amazing how life takes you on some unexpected journeys that bring losses, wins, and joy. No matter how you get a win as you travel along in life, it is the little wins that add up.

There was a time when I was injured in an accident and was not given a great diagnosis. I told the doctor, "Okay, well I'm going to check in with God because He is the ultimate physician." That journey required me to get in my own corner and fight so I could get little wins and find joy in the healing process. Do not be afraid to pursue or fight for what you want in life, health, and business!

For me, boxing is the greatest sport because of the mental acuity, stamina and endurance fighters have in their journey to become a Champion. Fighters know that they will get hit while moving forward and knocked down but remembers those wins along the journey will help them get back up.

Every successful person knows that to have success you have to fight. And if you are unwilling to train, you stand a chance in getting knocked out of this game called life. There are a lot of winners, but everyone remembers the pursuit and success of a Champion. You choose – winner or champion; there is a difference.

Affirmation: I am a Champion. Now, say it and mean it;

I AM A CHAMPION!

JOYCE WRIGHT

Joyce Wright is a Mother, Grandmother, and Customer Service Manager. She loves serving the Lord.

Explore Gods Divine Pleasure

You will show me the path of life; In your presence is fullness of joy and at thy right hand are pleasures forevermore. Psalm 16:11

"I am sad. I feel so burdened. My heart is so heavy right now. It is like the weight of the whole world is on my shoulders. When I look around, all I see are things that cause me pain. Oh, my life, oh my soul! Is there any hope for me?" Do these words sound familiar? Yes! There is still hope for you! Follow my guidelines carefully and you will discover where God hides all of His bountiful joy. The secret is private worship. Private worship means spending private time worshiping and praising God. As you do this, all the heaviness in your heart will be lifted, you will just discover that your burden has been eased off and you feel so light. Try this today. Starting might be tricky but push yourself to do it, and you will discover the unlimited joy in God's presence as you learn to worship Him privately.

Prayer: Lord Jesus, the special grace to worship you privately and to have a personal relationship with you, please grant unto me in Jesus's name.

SHURVONE WRIGHT

Shurvone Wright is a transformative leader, Coach, Best Selling Author, and Speaker. She is passionate about helping women transition when they are faced with a life event that will change the course of their life.

His Vision, His Provision

"For I know the plans I have for you" declares the Lord. "Plans to prosper you, and not harm you, plans to give you hope and a future." Jeremiah 29:11

Have you ever taken a leap of faith in your career, moved to another state, or started your own business? You have everything in place to make the move to the new career. You move to another state or start your own business and then it hits you. The feeling of fear or uncertainty tries to grip you and keep you stuck and second-guessing yourself. Fear starts to tell you things will not work out, that little voice in your head asks you repeatedly, "Who do you think you are?" During my transition from a 30-year nursing career to starting my own financial practice, it was the scariest thing I have ever done, but the most rewarding leap of faith move I have ever done. Fear tried to keep me down and doubt my decision, but God's grace and mercy sustained me. I was scared at the time, but I always knew God would make a way for me to accomplish my dreams and be successful. He does not give us a vision without the provision to see it to fruition. The provision can be in the form of money, support, guidance, and wisdom. If you have dreams and visions do not fear, God has you in His hand. He will direct you. He will send you support and lift you up in those times you need it most. So, NEVER GIVE UP. Trust God and know that He will complete what He started in you.

ATSILA YONA

Atsila Yona is a 23-year-old Author, Business Owner, and Researcher.

I Can See Clearly Now

You are altogether beautiful, my darling; there is no flaw in you.
Song of Songs 4:7

I can see now that I am all that I need. You came into my world saying you would set me free, but all you did was abuse me; emotionally, physically, and sexually. You told me you loved me, but you had your mindset to hurt me from the beginning. What you called love was really neglect. I yelled out into the world, but no one cared because they saw me as another debt. Calling out to family members but they do not care for my safety. Now, I am living in these strangers' homes hoping they will let me stay because I do not want to end up in a homeless shelter. Home after home, they kicked me out or I left willingly. I would rather be by myself than to be oppressed. I wished Mama would have protected me. My life would not be such a mess. Now I am stuck with anger, bitterness, and regrets. Coming into work every day, pretending to be happy when I am tired of being strong. I want to end it all. But if I kill myself, I will be giving my enemies just what they want; to see me fall. I cannot give up, but I cannot stop thinking. Was leaving home worth leaving? Yes! I had every right to do what is best for me. My battles made me wiser. I made it this far without needing the people who do not want to see me succeed. I am proud of how far I come. I know now that all I need is God and myself.

ODESSA YOUNG

Odessa Young is a Wife, Mother, and child of God. She is a Licensed Professional Counselor/Herbalife Wellness Coach who specializes in the mental health and overall wellness of her community one person at a time.

Survived by Grace

And He said unto me, "My grace is sufficient for thee: for my strength is made perfect in weakness." Most gladly, therefore, will I rather glory in my infirmities, that the power of Christ may rest upon me. 2 Corinthians 12:9

I walked down the paths of confusion avenue, shame boulevard, guilt street, and resentment circle. I pondered and asked for death at the intersection of abuse and abandonment. My life was altered by vicious events I experienced far too early in life. My dreams were distorted, tainted, and almost died before I had a chance to live.

I learned the value of education and love in an environment of chaos and confusion. I designed a plan in my mind to leave the old life behind in search of a new one. My heart was broken, shattered, healed, and made whole.

My joy and peace reside in the hands of my King who created me. I die daily and leave behind pieces of my old self I can no longer carry with me on this journey. I checked in my emotional baggage at the airport called "I will have a great future." My life will continue to unfold as I seek to be one percent better each day I live. My story will be shared, talked about to others, and repeated long after I depart from this place. I not only made it, I have survived by GRACE. Life has taught me I survived it all to live, to bring light to a dark world, and hope to the hopeless. May your life continue to be blessed and your strength always be enough to carry the load you will have to bear.   God's   grace   is   sufficient.

Printed in the United States of America by KDP

Publishing by PublishU©

Copyright 2020 by Vernessa Blackwell©

ISBN 978-0-9601043-1-4

Scriptures adapted from;

King James Version

New King James Version

New International Version

Good News Bible

Amplified Bible Classic Edition

Brandy Hunt

Publishu00@gmail.com

Facebook.com/Publish